Adolphus Julius Frederick Behrends

The Old Testament under Fire

Adolphus Julius Frederick Behrends

The Old Testament under Fire

ISBN/EAN: 9783337252830

Printed in Europe, USA, Canada, Australia, Japan

Cover: Foto ©Lupo / pixelio.de

More available books at **www.hansebooks.com**

THE OLD TESTAMENT UNDER FIRE

BY

A. J. F. BEHRENDS, DD., S.T.D.

PASTOR OF THE CENTRAL CONGREGATIONAL CHURCH
BROOKLYN, N. Y.

NEW YORK
FUNK & WAGNALLS COMPANY
LONDON AND TORONTO
1897

Dedicated to the Members of the Central Congregational Church and Society,

whose cordial support and earnest love for the Scriptures have been a constant source of courage and inspiration, through a ministry of more than fourteen years, by the author, who considers it his highest honor to be their Pastor

PREFACE.

THE contents of this little book were struck off at white heat. They were prepared to meet a pressing emergency, without any thought of publication. The author has yielded to the pressure of many friends, to give them more permanent form. He is fully aware that this volume can answer only a passing demand. He is not so blind as to suppose that it will take rank with the discussions of scholars. The several papers were prepared for audiences composed of intelligent and thoughtful men and women, who were fully competent to follow a close and searching argument, so long as the discussion was not swamped by technical details. To such readers, clerical and lay, they are submitted. Only the salient points are considered. And the free conversational style has been retained, as best suited to the purpose, which the author had in view.

The first chapter appeared, three years ago, in three articles, in the "*Christian Advocate*," of New York, and is reprinted with the consent of its editor. The remaining chapters are recent.

A. J. F. BEHRENDS.

96 Brooklyn Ave.,
   Brooklyn, N. Y.

TABLE OF CONTENTS

CHAPTER I
PAGE
GENERAL SURVEY 9–46

CHAPTER II
OUR LORD'S USE OF THE OLD TESTAMENT 47–62

CHAPTER III
CHRIST AND THE OLD TESTAMENT 63–95

CHAPTER IV
CRITICISM AND THE OLD TESTAMENT . . 96–147

CHAPTER V
CRITICISM AND COMMON SENSE 148–191

CHAPTER VI
THE HISTORIC FAITH 192–211

CHAPTER VII
THE INTEGRITY OF THE NEW TESTAMENT 212–240

NOTE 241–246

The Old Testament Under Fire

CHAPTER I.

GENERAL SURVEY.

"Hold fast that which thou hast."
REV. iii : 11.

I BEG to say, at the outset, that I do not pose as a specialist. I have only a running acquaintance with the language in which the ancient Scriptures were written, sufficient for the purpose of forming an independent judgment, but not warranting acceptance on my part of the challenge of debate. I am even less concerned to appear as a defender of the Bible. The ark of God is not in danger. Moses and the prophets are too deeply imbedded in the life of modern history, ever to be eliminated from it by the analytics of criticism. The discovery of new truth can result only in good; and he who deprecates or denounces criticism has already surrendered his faith, and has labeled himself the disciple of a blind traditionalism.

It is not an argument, therefore, which I propose to conduct. I am going to rise in my place and tell my experience, the resultant conviction to which several years of patient and painstaking study have led me. My readers must excuse, therefore, the frequent use of the personal pronoun, which in the present case is really an evidence of modesty. There came a time when I could no longer take my opinions at second hand from the critical specialists. Their differences among themselves were so many and so serious, that the only escape from either agnosticism, or a slavish following, lay in independent research. That involved, as preparatory, the careful and repeated reading of the Old Testament in Hebrew. The price was a heavy one, for one who had become rusty in the old Semitic tongue; but it must be ungrudgingly paid by every man who would be sure of his ground. The problems which criticism raises must not and can not be left to specialists. They must be canvassed by the men who occupy the pulpits, that they may speak with authority, though never with ostentation. They will be least obtruded into preaching by those who are most familiar with them. Still, the call of the hour is for preachers who can and do read the Hebrew of the Old Testament, as readily and habitually as they read the Greek of the New. And the men who do that, should and will preach the simplest Gospel.

CRITICISM LARGELY CONJECTURAL.

One thing which the last eight years have taught me is that the questions which criticism raises cannot be settled by mere argument. Demonstration is out of the question. Probability is all that can be reached, and in the logic of probability much depends upon pre-suppositions, and upon the personal peculiarities of the critic. There are no perfect eyes—some are even color-blind. There are no perfect ears—tones which to some are distinct and sweet may be faint and unmusical to others. There are no perfect critics —every man brings his temperament to the task.

This is true of even textual criticism. Tischendorf and Tregelles do not agree in their estimate of the relative importance of the ancient manuscripts. The text of the New Testament must remain uncertain so long as the original autographs are beyond our reach, and every intelligent Greek reader will exercise his liberty in the choice of renderings. The variations are confessedly of no practical importance, but they serve to show that there is considerable margin for the exercise of personal ingenuity and judgment. What convinces one man will not convince another, and an authoritative dictum cannot be reached. Much less can such a finality be reached in the literary criticism of the Biblical documents. The principles of literary criticism have never been formulated. Where the attempt has been made, the results have often been squarely set aside by the facts. Genius has many moods, and does not work in a mechanical harness. Sometimes it crawls, and then suddenly it rises upon wings of power. Its vocabulary is not always the same. Its style changes. It shifts the point of observation. Its products are not of the same grade. Different readers will be attracted by different tones. Some will regard this, others will regard that, as distinctive and peculiar. The critic always carries his own tastes to the task of analysis and comparison. Long lists of words, peculiarities of style, philosophical or theological colorings, are always more or less uncertain as data of impregnable conclusions.

Hence, literary criticism has always revealed a wide margin of conjecture. Its theories have been working hypotheses, often overthrown when they seemed to have been firmly established. Some claim that the style of the Elohist is easiest of detection; others think that the style of the Jahvist has been preserved in the greatest purity; others, again, contend that the Redactor has tampered with all styles, and made up a literary mosaic which makes it impossible to bring perfect order out of the confusion. Our work is reduced to happy guesses. And when this latter theory is maintained, simple-minded readers will conclude that the mysterious and mischievous Redactor may have been the original author, and not a compiler of separate and divergent documents, so that it might have been Moses, as well as any one else. Literary criticism is not so simple a matter as it seems to be. It bristles with conjectures. It is far from being strictly scientific. Personality has its hidden and unfathomable depths. The stronger the personality, the more varied will be its expression. It is never safe to predict what another man may do, and how he will do it; nor what he will say, and how he will say it. We must understand all his susceptibilities and moods, and all their possible combinations; and this cannot be done *a priori*. The man must be judged by what he has done or written; he cannot first be measured, and his writings sifted and separated under the assumed formula. Time, too, must be taken into account. Half a century may completely revolutionize a man's style; and a change of work may produce the same result. Grant was a soldier, and Chief Magistrate of the nation. But his military orders and reports are very different from his inaugural addresses and annual messages. It would not be hard to prove that General Grant and President Grant could not have been the same person; but the learned criticism would be laughed out of court.

At present the argument from style is held in abeyance, and regarded as only supplementary; the appeal is to variety of contents and to difference in conception. As if a poet could not write prose, and a prose author could not write poetry. Coleridge did both well. A man may be learned in the law, and be able also to make a popular address. The transition from one theme to another, with the inevitable accompaniment of a change in vocabulary, does not prove the agency of different authors. The point in all this is simply, that literary criticism is so largely subjective and conjectural, that one may be excused for shrugging his shoulders when it becomes dogmatic and censorious.

CRITICAL PROBLEMS INSOLUBLE.

A second lesson which I have learned, is that while the present problems of the Old Testament are perfectly legitimate, their satisfactory solution is something which need not be looked for. No new Bible will be the outcome. Agreed as most critics are as to the quartet of documents in the Hexateuch, they are not sure of their original form and contents. Not one of them, we are told, exists in its original integrity and completeness. The Redactor has scissored them all. Not only are there four imperfect documents, but each document has been compiled from many sources, which is declared to be pre-eminently true of the Priest-code. Nor are the critics agreed as to the date and the relative antiquity of the documents. The older scholars placed the Elohist first, but the present school makes him the last in the line; and the inversion compels the claim, that the poem of creation is an introduction to Genesis, added by the latest of the great unknown four, or by their editor.

The second chapter of Genesis is supposed to contain a duplicate account of the creation, and the history of the deluge is dissected as proving that two descriptions have been bunglingly united. It may provoke a smile from some specialists, but honesty compels me to say that, while I have no prejudice against the analysis, the arguments advanced have not convinced me. The first and second chapters of Genesis do not seem to me to contain duplicate accounts of the creation. The second chapter is an advance upon the first. Professor Green appears to me to have fully answered President Harper. And I can discover no such contradictions or variations in the account of the deluge, as is assumed and maintained. This may be because I am not a specialist, and am lacking in literary tact; but the independent reader will have to be taken into account, if the specialist expects to give currency to his analysis. What has been said of exegesis is true of criticism, which is only a branch of exegesis, that its correctness must be determined by the intelligent consensus of Christendom.

More than this. The literary criticism of the Old Testament has ceased to trouble me, because I have a strong conviction that the problem upon which it is at work is hopelessly insoluble. The history of New Testament criticism affords an instructive example. The synoptic problem is the most intricate and fascinating of all questions of the later Biblical literature. Every possible combination has been suggested; the most exact and exhaustive analysis has been made; and the result is failure along the whole line. There is only conjecture; and the simplest theory is as good as any, that the gospels are independent of each other, though resting upon a common tradition, and that the sources from which they were compiled cannot now be tabulated. The authors have not given us their authorities, and we cannot make good the literary omission.

The composition of the Pentateuch is a problem of tenfold greater difficulty. It lies much farther away from our time. We have no other writings of similar traditional antiquity with which to compare it. Its Mosaic authorship was once denied on the ground that the age was illiterate, and that writing was unknown. But recent discoveries in the valleys of the Nile and the Euphrates, have exploded that assumption. Unless Moses be resolved into a purely mythical figure, he must have known how to write; and the consciousness of his peculiar vocation would have impelled him to write. How much did he write? What documents, and how many, did he have in his possession? Who can tell? He has not told us; and if he did not write a line, the men who did write the documents have not affixed their names, and they have not told us whence they derived their information. A modern writer takes pains to tell us what authorities he has consulted, and adds numerous notes to the text. But the Pentateuch has neither note nor appendix. Nearly twenty-five hundred years have passed since the Exile; and if Ezra knew anything of these matters he has given no sign. Take any modern book, with all contemporary literature at our command, but with no quotation marks or confessions of indebtedness, would not the literary analysis of its sources be a task of great difficulty? But the sources of the Hexateuch and of the historical books have no independent existence. Comparison cannot be made. Such documents as existed have long since perished. Is it not a Gordian knot which the critics are trying to unravel, and who is the Alexander that he should cut the knot with the sword, and then claim that he had untied it? Apart from tradition, the literary problem is insoluble; and the only question of importance is whether the record as it stands, bears upon it the stamp of general truthfulness.

LITERARY CRITICISM SUBORDINATE TO HISTORICAL.

The third lesson which I have learned is, that the literary criticism of the Biblical documents is, in grave and essential importance, subordinate to the historical criticism of their contents. In fact, literary criticism may almost be said to have become the servant of historical criticism. The crucial question is, whether the Old Testament is substantially correct in the account which it gives of the rise and development of true religion, and of its culmination in the Messiah of law and psalm and prophecy. And here, there is a subtle quality in its literary substance and form, which wins my confidence the more familiar I become with it. It is pervaded by a high ethical tone. It does not picture ideal heroes. It sketches the shame as well as the glory, and both with literary simplicity. It exalts the veracity of God—His personal veracity as holiness, and His veracity in dealing with men, as remembering and keeping His covenant. The prophets never flatter. They speak words of truth and soberness. A lying history could not have been written by men breathing such an atmosphere. Be the difficulties of harmonizing what they may, were they tenfold greater than they are, they do not and could not compare with the monstrosity of a forged and false history, issuing from men who hated and denounced lying.

But more. One thing criticism has been forced to grant: There was a Moses. His was the commanding and creative personality. He planted the acorn, if he did not create the wide-branching tree. The theology and the ritual of the Old Testament bear his impress. There was an ark, and a tent, and sacrifices, and a written law, before there was a temple. Monotheism was not a product of the prophetic era. It was present and active from the very first, though only in germ, as a religious force rather than a theological dogma, and though it required many centuries and many a severe struggle to give it exclusive and universal ascendancy. So much stands, whatever reconstruction of the history is ventured upon. The nation was right when it said: "Abraham is our father, and Moses our lawgiver." And, with so much granted, a good deal more will have to be yielded. The revolutionary criticism seems to have reached its limits, and it is already retreating to a more moderate position, where the prophets will not be left without a theological ancestry, and where the second temple will not be made the creation of Ezekiel's fancy and of Ezra's manipulation.

UNWARRANTABLE ASSUMPTIONS OF DESTRUCTIVE CRITICISM.

The fourth lesson which I have learned is, that historical criticism of the Old Testament, so far as its results are revolutionary and destructive, proceeds upon utterly unwarrantable assumptions. It denies the reality of supernatural revelation and guidance. It sneers at miracles, and discredits any history which contains them. It resolves predictions into happy guesses, or regards them as uttered *post eventum*. It claims that, where a law is generally disregarded and violated, the statute could not have existed. It insists that a steady upward evolution is the universal law of history, and that Israel therefore could not have fallen from monotheism into idolatry, but must have risen from fetichism into monotheism. Taking so much for granted, the attempt to prove the recorded history misleading and incredible is a needless task.

But every one of these assumptions is unscientific, and is discredited by history. Revelation is a permanent feature of life, as our ethical intuitions and religious aspirations prove. Conscience is the mightiest of forces, supporting the authority of moral law as uncreated and eternal; and conscience and moral law bring all life into living contact with the supernatural and spiritual. God is immanent in the life of the world. Theism granted, and miracles are possible, while the resurrection of Jesus Christ blocks the path of every man, who ventures upon their universal rejection. All history is luminous with ethical ideals which have been widely disregarded. The golden rule is not even now obeyed; did not Christ then utter the words? And is it true that an unbroken line of upward development is the story which history tells? Its pages are full of the record of political and religious apostasies. The early days of Greece were the best. The first centuries of Rome were the brightest. Primitive Christianity was better than its mediæval type, and our theological reformers make the cry, "Back to Christ," their watchword. The record of the Old Testament religion corresponds, in its broad outlines, to the general history of the world, a constant and fierce battle, a succession of apostasies and reformations. Destructive criticism discredits its own results by its unhistorical and unscientific assumptions; and as the foundations are laid in the quicksand, the elaborate superstructure is doomed to collapse without the cost and the fatigue of bombardment. When historical criticism ceases to make its conclusions the premises of its argument, it will be time enough to take it seriously.

CHARGES OF LITERARY FORGERY.

I pass to a fifth point. If the philosophical postulates of destructive criticism are unscientific and unhistorical, the conscious and wholesale literary immorality which it charges upon the

Biblical writers, provokes the resentment of every fair-minded student. It would not be so bad if the literature were evaporated into romance. But it is branded as counterfeit, and as deliberately reversing the order of facts, as transferring to ancient times what was an afterthought and a late priestly invention. Deuteronomy is declared not to have been found in Josiah's reign by Hilkiah, but to have been written by him, and palmed off upon the king and the nation, as a credible record of what Moses said and commanded in the plains of Moab. We are told that this pious act must not be condemned as forgery, because literary methods were not as strict as they now are, and that wholesale plagiarism was universally practised; that speeches were credited to men which they never uttered, and which only represented what the author imagined they might or must have said; and that the emergency which confronted Josiah was such, that extraordinary measures were required to meet it. But we look in vain, through the ethics of the prophetical literature, which confessedly was in existence at that time, for any intimation that the end justifies the means. Every prophet would have denounced the maxim; and this prophetic environment makes it incredible that so stupendous a literary invention, upon which the political fortunes of so many depended, could have been undertaken and carried forward to success. The audacity of the priest amazes one, and the stupidity of the people passes comprehension. Was there no way of determining whether Hilkiah's roll was an old or a new one? It was not kept under lock and key. It was read not only to Shaphan, the scribe, as a co-conspirator, but also to the king, who was not let into the secret, and then to large public assemblies which the king summoned. Friends and foes of the reform movement were present, saw, and heard, and not a voice was lifted against the solemn covenant which was publicly entered into over this roll which Hilkiah had produced; and yet it was all an invention! Seriously, what shall be said of such historical criticism?

Much in the same way the middle books of the Pentateuch are declared to be a post-exilian product, the work of an ambitious priesthood, who dressed up their ordinances in the literary garments of the wilderness life, to give them easy currency among the people, and then invented the whole series of patriarchal stories as a fitting imaginary introduction. Moses cannot be regarded as the author even of the Decalogue. To admit that, would involve the high antiquity of the first chapter of Genesis. The Psalter is brought down bodily to the period of the second temple, and David vanishes from its pages altogether. Joel cannot possibly be allowed a place among the older prophets, because his testimony to the ancient ritual is too varied and explicit. Chronicles is a priestly fabrication throughout, and wholly unworthy of credence. If similar passages are found in Judges and Kings, subtle, artless, and undesigned coincidences, they are quietly checked off as interrupting the narrative, introducing irrelevant ideas, and interpolations by an unknown priestly redactor. Such critical judgments would be strange enough if the books in question were only private pamphlets, having a narrow and official circulation. But the hypothesis is a most monstrous one, when it is applied to documents which constituted a popular literature, which passed into many hands and were freely circulated, and which were divided into pericopes and regularly read in a thousand synagogues. As well suppose that *Robinson Crusoe* and the *Arabian Nights* will ever be read in our churches with the gospels and the epistles. The theory brings the indictment of forgery against the entire nation, a supposition so violent that it needs only to be plainly stated, to be instantly and indignantly rejected. The nation's imprimatur will count for something with every reader, who has no particular theory to defend. He may find difficulties and discrepancies, as he does in any similar historical record, but he cannot regard the entire literature a lie.

The tortuous way in which even moderately conservative critics deal with Hilkiah's discovery of Deuteronomy, has a tendency to create a profound distrust of the literary ethics of the critical procedure. Canon Driver and Professor Briggs shrink from the plain charges of forgery preferred by Kuenen and Wellhausen, but they save the honesty of the main actors in the scene, only by somewhat minimizing their crime, and by the use of dexterous phrases, which they imagine convert the procedure into something legitimate and praiseworthy. Canon Driver intimates that the kernel of Deuteronomy is old and of Mosaic origin, but that its "parenetic setting" belongs to the age of Josiah, and that it may be described as the "prophetic reformulation and adaptation to new needs of an older legislation." Professor Briggs is somewhat more blunt, when he says that Hilkiah is not the author of the Deuteronomic Code, but of "a new codification of an ancient code," of an ancient code which was found, and which after its discovery was cast into a new historical form. His theory is that "an ancient Mosaic code was discovered in Josiah's time, and that the code was put into popular rhetorical form, as a people's law book for practical purposes, under the authority of king, prophet, and priest."

This, we are told, we are at liberty to "*suppose.*" Certainly, and we may suppose a great many more things, without a scintilla of evidence, and squarely in the face of the record. The roll, whatever it may have contained, is said to have been found, and to have been read, *as found*, to Shaphan, to the king, and to the people. There is no intimation of a recodification, or of the addition of a new " parenetic setting." It does not help the matter to say that the literary forgery was only in the dress. Coin is none the less counterfeit because it contains a little genuine metal. If we may suppose that the parenetic setting was invented, why must we suppose the code to have been ancient? Whatever date may be assigned to Deuteronomy, assuming Hilkiah's roll to have been the original Deuteronomy — which cannot be proved — it would seem to be clear that there cannot be any middle ground between its being a wholesale literary fraud, and its discovery in its present form in Josiah's reign. Its present "parenetic setting" may have been given to it long after Moses, but to regard the "parenetic setting" as a later literary artifice, and the attempt to associate that setting with the discovery of an ancient code by Hilkiah, is substantially a surrender to Wellhausen. It is not so intended ; but plain men will not be able to make anything else out of it. The critics mean well, but they show a strange ethical twist, when they deceive themselves by phrases and conjectures, whose emptiness appears as soon as they are stripped of their rhetoric.

RECENT LEADERS OF THE MEDIATING SCHOOL.

The deserved prominence of Professor Briggs as a Biblical critic, and the wide attention which his utterances and trial have commanded, justify a brief reference to his last book as outlining his present position. In it he professes to have given the results of twenty-seven years of critical study, and Christian scholarship had a right to expect as strong and conclusive an argument as it was possible for him to give. Candor compels me to say that the reader is doomed to bitter disappointment, and can only close the volume with the certain conviction that the author has not solved the problems of Old Testament criticism. The book is a strange medley, consisting of several documents of earlier publication, which have been amended, expanded, or contracted, with numerous interpolations of sentences and paragraphs, and with equally numerous reversals of previous judgments. It is practically an abandonment of the conservative ground which the author held ten years before, a conservatism which at that time was regarded as dangerous liberalism. At that earlier period he had already occupied a professor's chair for fourteen years, and had been a specialist in Old Testament studies for seventeen years. He had mastered the literature of the whole subject, and the theories of Graf, Kuenen, and Wellhausen had long been familiar to scholars. Ten years before the date of his last book, his judgment of the composition and authorship of the Pentateuch was stated in these words: "There is nothing in the variation of the documents, as such, to require that they should be successive and separated by wide intervals, or that would prevent their being very nearly contemporaneous. There is nothing in the distinction of the documents, as such, that forbids the Mosaic age as the time of their origin."

On the date of Deuteronomy, Professor Briggs declared in 1883, that De Wette's theory was "exceedingly precarious." He claimed to have disproved, against De Wette, the location of

Deuteronomy in the age of Josiah, and to have shown that its origin must be thrown back into the Mosaic age. As to the post-exilian origin of the Priest-code he maintained that there were "insuperable objections" to such a theory, and he presented his reasons in detail. He admitted the *order* of development, for which Kuenen and Wellhausen contended — a most vicious concession — but he denied "that it was necessary to postulate a thousand years for this development," and he suggested that "if we should suppose that Eleazar or some other priest gathered these detailed laws and groups of laws into a code at the time subsequent to the conquest, all the conditions of variation and development might be explained."

Between this, and the contention of 1893, the gulf is deep and wide. The last book displays no greater learning than the earlier essays, and in logical vigor it is decidedly inferior. His last volume has certainly not added to his reputation. Its learning is undigested. The material is chaotic. The tone of argument is not judicial. There is a painful want of logical clearness and consistency. Ingenious suggestions take the place of proof. Dangerous and revolutionary theories are modified by a personal caveat. Their logical issue is simply evaded. Names are made to take the place of evidence. The reader is overawed by a list of authorities, in which all schools are indiscriminately jumbled together. The counter arguments are in the main ignored, and conservative critics are labeled in schoolboy fashion. The reader who can divest himself of prejudice, lays down the book with the feeling that, if this is the best that can be said, the problem has not even been clearly stated, and that its solution is a long way off. And the same judgment must be passed upon Canon Driver's book, which Professor Briggs speaks of as "invaluable," many a page of which bristles with assumptions for which not the slightest evidence is given. The critical processes are reverential in spirit, but they are very far from being severely scientific; and the historical criticism is thoroughly loose and arbitrary. The traditional view of the origin of the present Pentateuch may require modification, but the present mediating school cannot be said to have defended the credibility of the Old Testament, and its claim to being the record of a divine revelation, against the assaults of the destructive critics.

Perhaps one of the fairest specimens of the present mediating school, which seeks to retain the divine authority of the Old Testament as a gradually unfolding religious revelation, while regarding the literature as a late production, largely composed of mythical and legendary elements, and worthless in many parts as historical material, is the treatise on *Old Testament Theology*, by Dr. Hermann Schultz, of Göttingen, a work now accessible to English readers. The tone is calm and the spirit is reverent. The reality of a divine revelation in the production of the ancient faith is conceded and maintained, as demanded by the conditions of the problem to be solved. Monotheism in a religious form is affirmed to have been the pre-Mosaic faith in Israel, though Moses did much to give it prominence, while the prophets are credited with giving it theological form. The deliverance from the bondage of Egypt is regarded as a historical fact, as everywhere assumed, inextricably interwoven with all the subsequent history, though the miracles are passed over in silence. Moses cannot be a myth. He is not the author of the Decalogue in its present form, because the stern prohibition against the use of images in divine worship points unmistakably to a later period, though in some form the Ten Commandments must be acknowledged as the basis of his legislation. There was an ark which was sheltered by a tent, though the tabernacle is the creation of later poetic fancy; its description being "not a delineation of an actual thing, but a depicting of religious thoughts borrowed from Solomon's temple." The presence of the ark gave to Israel from the first a national sanctuary, outranking in dignity all local altars, and in that sanctuary no image ever found a place, though the exclusive dignity of the sacred shrine which contained the ark, dates from a much later period, to which David, Solomon, and other kings, contributed. The tribe of Levi is conceded to have been a priestly class from the beginning, though not to the exclusion of other individuals, and without such an organization as appears in the middle books of the Pentateuch. Sacrifice is an early institution. The feasts of Tabernacles and of the Passover are of Mosaic origin. Circumcision is a pre-Mosaic custom and religious in its meaning, as a consecration of life to God.

This hasty review shows how much the historical analysis feels constrained to grant, as a basis upon which the great prophetic era must rest. The edifice of the ninth century before Christ, as represented by the older prophets and by Isaiah, and by the cultus of the Exile, must have some solid foundation in the ancient era. The argument is unanswerable, and its lines have been skillfully followed by Professor Robertson, of Glasgow. But it is hard to see how Schultz can concede so much, while contending that the literature of the Old Testament is trustworthy only as showing what was believed when that literature was produced, and that it cannot be relied upon as a historical record. The concessions are at war with the criticism. It is only an individual opinion which remains, unsupported by documentary evidence, and such an opinion can have no authority. Every man is at liberty to apply the brakes anywhere, or to refuse applying them anywhere. Whatever the picture of the Mosaic age, it must be drawn from the literature as it now exists, a literature which, as a whole, is discredited by Schultz as much as it is by Wellhausen. That literature is confessedly homogeneous, as even Ewald insisted; and it would seem that if the literature is false *in totis*, it cannot be reliable *in singulis*. Some, with Vernes, have taken that step, and declare that the entire history is legendary, and that the Mosaic era must remain for us a splendid national myth. And, to me at least, the herculean labors of the mediating school seem to be an attempt to arrest Niagara by a dam of straw.

REAL DIFFICULTIES OF BIBLICAL CRITICISM.

The difficulties and the discrepancies which emerge in a critical examination of the Scripture records, are connected with the minor details of the narrative, and with the fragmentary nature of the literature in which the history has been preserved. One peculiarity of that literature is that it is prophetic, not photographic. It seizes upon the great outstanding facts in which the divine discipline of the race, and especially of the chosen people, is most clearly manifest, and by which the preparation for the advent of Jesus Christ is most signally illustrated. The Bible is written in a large way, not in the method of minute descriptive and chronological completeness. We are conducted over a series of mountain peaks, while the broad intervening valleys are left shrouded in mist and gloom. The lives of the patriarchs are fragmentary sketches. The bondage in Egypt occupies only a paragraph. We look in vain for a biography of Moses, whose personal discipline of eighty years must have had an important bearing upon his subsequent public career. The story reads abruptly, but the abruptness is due to the silence which covers the formative years. Thirty-eight years of the wilderness life are passed over in silence, and we might argue from the silence that they are a legendary addition, while, if the silence were removed, the lost background of the priestly legislation might be recovered. Judges, Samuel and Kings do not furnish complete histories. Here and there we come upon sharp and severe conflicts between monotheism and idolatry, without any intimation as to the relative strength of the opposing parties, and without any sketch of the intervening periods. Even when altars multiplied, and sacrifices were offered on a hundred heights, a central sanctuary remained, with its tabernacle and ark and altar, as in Samuel's time, and in the period of the kings. The ritual in use is not described; but the same silence characterizes the mention of idolatrous forms of worship, though we know that these were in charge of a priesthood, and must have been associated with a regular and imposing ceremonial. There was always a remnant which resisted the popular current, and that remnant always appealed to ancient usage. Royal authority might seize the temple and corrupt the priesthood and ignore the ancient feasts; but the fact that repeated attempts were made to correct these abuses, proves that the remembrance of the older order never wholly perished.

If in Elijah's time, when Ahab and Jezebel ruled in Samaria, seven thousand had not bowed the knee to Baal, we may confidently presume that much larger numbers retained the primitive faith under better kings. The fact that royal authority so often, and for such long periods, stood in the way of a general and orderly observance of the appointed feasts and sacrifices, does not prove that there existed universal ignorance of an ancient and Mosaic ritual, much less that such a ritual had never been instituted. The fragmentariness of the record deprives the argument from silence of its adverse weight, and the final triumph of the monotheistic doctrine, and of the centralized ritual, implies their presence from the earliest stages of the religious conflict. That there should be variant accounts of the long periods, as when Chronicles and Kings are compared, is not surprising, when we bear in mind that no writer has given a complete account of any single event or reign; and hence, to pit Judges and Samuel against the Pentateuch, and Kings against Chronicles, and the prophets against the Priest-code, is a thoroughly unscientific procedure. That there are difficulties in harmonizing the accounts is freely granted, and the task of historical reconstruction is not an easy one ; but the problem is certainly not solved by arraying the records against each other, by throwing the accessible materials into inextricable confusion, and by charging the writers with manipulating and even inventing the facts in support of their theories.

Similar difficulties confront us in harmonizing the evangelistic narratives, and in reproducing the exact history of the early Church. The gospels and the Acts are fragmentary records, and leave many questions unanswered. If we had only the Synoptists, we might conclude that our Lord's public ministry lasted only a single year. The fourth gospel compels us to adopt a different chronology. There are varying reports of the same miracles, of the Lord's Prayer, of the Sermon on the Mount, and of Christ's dying utterances. The different accounts of the resurrection of our Lord cannot be harmonized. It was not within the range of human possibility to give a perfectly accurate or photographic description of so momentous an event. The resurrection itself, like the creation or incarnation, was an invisible and inscrutable miracle. No one saw the Crucified rising from the sepulcher. The agreement is perfect that Christ was seen after He had risen from the dead, and that is the only thing of importance. Who was first at the grave, and whether there were two angels or only one, are matters of insignificance. So, while there is general agreement between the narrative in Acts and in the Pauline epistles, there are minor details which present difficulties in completely harmonizing the different accounts. Such imperfections belong to all historical literature. Its credibility is limited to the general lines of movement; variant and even contradictory accounts appear as soon as unimportant details are brought into the story. There is no agreement as to the hour of day on which the battle of Waterloo was fought; *but Waterloo was fought.* There are square contradictions as to the place where Bismarck and Napoleon met at Sedan; *but Napoleon surrendered at Sedan.* The main fact is not discredited by the variant and even contradictory testimony concerning minor details. It would be easy, adopting the methods of the current Old Testament criticism, to discredit the entire traditional history of the Plymouth Colony, and to resolve it into an admixture of fact and fiction, by pitting the writings of Bradford against those of Winslow, and by showing that in some particulars Bradford's history is contradicted by his *Letter Book*.

GENERAL CREDIBILITY THE ONLY RESULT OF HISTORICAL CRITICISM.

General credibility—credibility in the main outlines—is all that can be demanded of historical and biographical literature. He who exacts more may as well turn his back upon all the historians, even the most painstaking and conscientious of them. Are we to look for anything more in an inspired writer? That question may be answered dogmatically in the affirmative. It may be assumed that the Biblical history must be complete and absolutely inerrant in every slightest detail. But the assumption is contradicted by the facts. There are incomplete and variant accounts, and thus far the differences have refused to melt together in the critical crucible. General credibility is all that we can claim, and, whether it suits our dogmatic position or not, we must be content with it. It certainly is a reversal of all scientific and sensible criticism, to seize upon the variations in the historical narrative, and by their use to discredit the entire record, and to reverse its general movement; as unreasonable and absurd as it would be to make the battle of Waterloo a fiction, or to convert Bismarck and Napoleon into legendary persons, because the accounts of different eye-witnesses do not agree. Few things are more important for the critical study of the Bible, than a liberal supply of downright common sense; and when historical criticism parts with common sense, applying tests to Scripture which would not be applied to any other historical literature, the critical results are discredited in advance. Variations in historical details ought not to be an obstacle to faith. They are watermarks of general veracity and evidence of independent testimony; they prove that there was no collusion. It may be that other and graver difficulties face us in Holy Scripture, as a trial to our faith, to purge it, to teach us the important lesson that the letter killeth, while only the spirit maketh alive. The Bible, after all, is the handbook of redemption. It tells us "how to go to heaven, not how the heavens go." It has been given us to make us wise unto salvation, and to perfectly equip us for every service in righteousness. This has been its great and mighty mission in the past, and the past is sufficient to vindicate its unique dignity and authority. That mission let us push with an undying ardor, until its message of hope has won all hearts, and made the face of the round earth radiant with its eternal joy!

CHAPTER II.

Our Lord's Use of the Old Testament.

> "Search the Scriptures; for in them ye think ye have eternal life; and they are they which testify of me."
> —John v : 39.

We are in the habit of speaking of an intelligent Christianity. I have used the phrase myself; and, if I live, I presume that I shall use it a good many times more. But the adjective is really superfluous. There is no such thing as an unintelligent Christianity. The Life is the Light of men. The moment we undertake to define Christianity in the simplest terms, that moment we must affirm propositions, and project problems, which demand the patient and strenuous exercise of the reason. And the reason is not satisfied, unless the answers given are stated in clear and unmistakable language. A vague theology is the sign of a decaying church, and is to be dreaded even more than a pedantic and hair-splitting scholasticism. I have no objection to a reconstructed theology; only I want it to be *theology*, definite, Scriptural, consistent. We are told that every age must do its own thinking. Agreed; but it should be *thinking*, not dreaming. In much of our current literature I miss definiteness. There is more and better rhetoric than in Jonathan Edwards; but there is much less, and much poorer, logic. There is more fog than light. The outlines are shadowy, and the substance vanishes when hands are laid upon it. The fathers are freely criticised; but empty balloons are substituted for their solid structures. I am sure that this cannot last; and many a volume, now praised as a valuable contribution to theological thought, will drop out of sight before its author has become invisible. I want clear thinking. The church and the world want it. And the very first evidence that we have ploughed through the fog which has settled down upon us, will be books in which things are said that the reader can understand, and pulpits which will preach the old gospel with the old incisiveness. It is high time that this work were begun. For myself, I must confess that I should starve if I had only the theologians of the last decade. I am glad the old are with me, and that the New Testament is in my hands. And I am afraid that the people in the pews are starving, because there is no clear-cut theology in the pulpit.

There may be — there are — religions in which the use of reason is needless, and even a hindrance; but Christianity is not one of them, and never has been. Its eternal life is grounded in the knowledge of God; not in speculative knowledge, nor in the sentimental agnosticism of our time, which is haughty with all its airs of humility, but in knowledge producing personal conviction, and realized in personal conduct. And the whole history of Christianity shows that wherever its message is heard and heeded, there it becomes at once, and continues to be, the leaven of intellectual, as well as of moral, ferment. It molds life, and it creates a literature. When the rational drops out, the religious vanishes.

CHRISTIANITY AND THE BIBLE.

So it comes to pass, that Christianity is prolific in the production of books. The oldest extant manuscripts are those of the Sacred Scriptures. The first book ever printed was the Bible. Christianity has sometimes been declared not to be the religion of a book. This is a very common statement, at present, and is proclaimed with an air of authority, as if it were a new discovery. It is one of the most threadbare of platitudes. Of course, a book must be thought out, before it can be written or printed. And it cannot be thought out in any real sense, unless it has been lived out. Life and thought must precede, and without them there will be no call for printing-presses and types. But the book is needed to preserve what has thus been experienced and thought out. In much of modern use, this harmless statement is meant to suggest that Christianity would remain, even if the Bible could be proved to be false from cover to cover. Our religion is declared to be independent of it. It is not. Its life is bound up with the reality of the facts recorded in the Testaments.

The famous saying of Chillingworth has been challenged, when he said: "The Bible, the Bible, is the religion of Protestants." We are reminded that Christianity is the religion of Christ; that it existed decades before a line of the New Testament was written; and that not a book, but a person, claims our confidence and allegiance. Chillingworth would have assented to all that. But he would have added "Christ was a historical person; His birth, His teachings, His miracles, His death, His resurrection, were historical events; and historical events can be known by us, only as we know Alexander, Cæsar, and Napoleon." There can be no Christ *in* history, if there was no Christ *of* history; and the latter can be known only by the use of the gospels and the epistles. This rigidly historical picture of Christ is the lungs and the heart of Christianity. No idealization can take its place. The church wants, and must have, the Christ into whose pierced side Thomas was summoned to thrust his hand. And the certainty of historical events can be preserved, and the knowledge of them can be communicated, only by written records. Tradition cannot be relied upon; the pen must fix what the eye has seen, and what the ear has heard. Thus the Book follows as a matter of absolute necessity, if we are not to be the victims of hopeless uncertainty. This is the office which the Scriptures perform for us, and which they have always performed.

CHRIST'S CHALLENGE TO THE PHARISEES.

In the passage at the head of this chapter, the Revised Version substitutes for the imperative form of the verb " search," the present tense of the indicative " ye search," placing the alternative reading in the margin. It is impossible to pronounce definitely upon this matter, and nothing of consequence is involved in it. The address of our Lord, in vindication of Himself and of His claims, culminates in the paragraph introduced by this sentence. He had healed a helpless paralytic, a cripple of thirty-eight years' standing, by a word. It was the Sabbath; and as the man walked home, carrying the bed on which he had been lying, he was met by indignant remonstrances. He could only answer that his unknown healer had commanded him to do what he was doing. He went his way; but his very next act was to repair to the temple, doubtless to give God thanks for his wonderful recovery, and perhaps also in the hope of meeting his deliverer. In this he was not disappointed, and so the Jews came to know that Jesus had made him whole. This aroused their indignation, and precipitated a bitter assault. The Jews sought to slay Jesus; and in His defense Christ exasperated them still more, because He claimed equality with God. He appealed to the miracle which He had wrought. He appealed to John, who had borne witness to Him. And finally, He appealed to the Scriptures, which His critics and enemies held in the highest reverence. He declared that if they believed the writings of Moses, they would believe in Him. Moses wrote of Him, and the Scriptures testified of Him. They agreed that the Scriptures declared the way of salvation, and that in consequence they were entitled to reverent and attentive examination. To that court Jesus made His final appeal, recognizing that even His claims must be reviewed in the light of their authority. He never ventured to set them aside, but declared that He had come to fulfill them. There are three things in our Lord's challenge which command attention.

THE SCRIPTURES OF CHRIST OUR BIBLE.

The first is, that there was a collection of writings, which passed under the name of "Scriptures," which were well-known, whose supreme authority He recognized and affirmed. It will always be a matter of great importance to Christians, to know what this collection was, upon which Christ set the stamp of His approval, and to whose authority He bowed. The question is one which admits of a definite answer, placed beyond all possibility of challenge. The collection included all that appears in our Old Testament, and in the very form in which it has come down to us. Twenty-one hundred years ago, the Canon of the Old Testament was just what it is now, as appears plainly from the Greek translation, completed at that time. So far as there has been, and is, any debate, it relates to the part which Ezra and his successors played in the formation of the collection, and how much farther back we may reasonably assume that such a collection existed. Ezra and his associates were only the latest and final editors, bringing the separate and scattered rolls together in critically authorized editions. No one pretends that they wrote the books, nearly twenty-five hundred years ago.

Here, then, is the one absolutely fixed point in the bewildering debate — that Christ read the same Old Testament which lies in our hands. The Pentateuch, the historical and prophetical books, the psalms, and other poetic pamphlets, existed in their present form when He lived. He had read them, and had heard them read; and He had mastered them as none had done until then, and as none have done since then. No one called their sacred authority in question. The nation recognized them as the Magna Charta of its liberty, the Divine constitution of the Theocracy, founded by Moses as the prophet of God. And Christ accepted this estimate of the Old Testament. For Him, too, these Scriptures could not be broken, and by their use He met and silenced His opponents. The Pharisees and the Devil alike, He smote with the sword of the Word of God. "*It is written,*" put them all to flight, and left Him master of the field.

Now, I do not wish to press this endorsement unduly. I am prepared to grant that it does not necessarily commit us to a literal interpretation of the Book of Jonah, nor to the allegorical view of the Song of Songs. There are a host of critical questions, connected with the composition and the transmission of the Old Testament writings, upon which Christ did not pass judgment; simply because they were not agitated in His day, and we have no reason to suppose that they were present to His mind. We must be content with what He did say, and not twist His words to mean more. He speaks, for instance, of the Psalter as David's; and yet He must have known that many psalms in the collection were declared to have been written by other men; for the inscriptions are certainly as old as the Canon of His time. The Psalter was the hymn-book of the Old Testament church, known as David's, because he gave the main impulse to its creation; just as we speak of the hymnals of Watts, and of Wesley, though these contain the hymns written by other men. He speaks of the Pentateuch as the work of Moses, Mosaic in inception, substance, and general scope, Mosaic in authority, though this does not involve the claim that

Moses himself wrote the whole of it. I am not disposed to invoke the authority of Christ upon problems of literary and historical criticism. He never assumed the role of a critic. He was too busy for that. He had more important work to do. He came to give His life a ransom for many. Would that we might follow in His steps, consumed with the holy passion for souls! The legitimacy of the most searching criticism may, and must, be conceded; but it is in point to call attention to its subordinate importance, and to the fact that the task is one of great difficulty; and it would be easy to mention the names of many men who, in twenty years, have completely reversed their former judgments, and have at last confessed their ignorance.

Under these circumstances, it is well to remember that there is one fixed point — Jesus Christ accepted the Old Testament as we have it; He accepted the whole of it, and nothing beside. This, for the Christian, will be decisive. The authority of Christ must be broken down, before the Scriptures of the Old Testament can be reduced to any lower rank than authoritative records and exponents of a Divine and historical revelation. And it is well to note, that this word *"Scripture"* or *"Scriptures"* is applied to the collection as a whole. It is in the plural, because the pamphlets are many; so that the conception of them as a *"library"* is by no means a modern discovery. This is one of the worn-out platitudes, by the way, which the new critics are fond of trotting out as something unheard of before. But the word is also in the singular, because the thirty-nine pamphlets are also thirty-nine chapters in a single book. This, the critics have not considered as they should. The Old Testament Scriptures are *"Scripture"* in the totality of their contents, in the consistency and balancing of all their parts. The authority is in the living unity of narrative, and precept, and doctrine, and prophecy.

SALVATION, THE BURDEN OF SCRIPTURE.

A second important thing in our Lord's challenge demands careful attention. It is this, that the value of the Old Testament is in its revelation of the Way of Salvation. Everything else is subordinate. The Scriptures disclose the nature, the necessity, the source, the conditions, the means, the present and future fruits, of eternal life. This is the study of them which our Lord commanded, and commended. I am not to go to them for my chronology, nor for my science, nor even for my history, but to be made wise unto salvation. That is the path upon which their light was made and meant to shine. And upon that path no other light does shine. The fearless application of this simple principle cannot fail to bring great relief. It will serve to keep us unmoved in the fiercest shock of the critical battle. For the warnings remain, the precepts remain, the promises remain; no matter by whom, or at what time, these were first believed, or uttered, or recorded. There is heaven in them, and heaven beyond them; and thereby they carry in and with them the sure evidence of their heavenly origin.

I may not know who fashioned this wondrous harp, by whom its strings were arranged, fastened, and tuned; I may not see the fingers which sweep over the chords; but I know that the music quiets my fears, and hushes my sorrows, and inspires me with hope. "*He that is born of God, hath the witness in himself,*" says John. And the same is true of those who read the Scriptures, that they may secure eternal life. They will have the witness in themselves, that these things are true. Let me add that our Lord's rule is a good one, not for general readers only, but also for ministers and experts. The Scriptures are only then studied aright, they are only then preached aright, when all critical processes, and all public expositions, are made to converge upon the clear exhibition of what they have to say about that salvation which is eternal life. "*We have this treasure in earthen vessels,*" said Paul. He referred to his preaching. But it is as true of the written word. The treasure of God is in an earthen vessel. That should make us careful of the vessel, for when that is shattered, the treasure may be lost to us. There may be what we deem flaws in it; still, to pick at these flaws until we puncture the vessel, is a very questionable procedure. But we shall also be wise enough to magnify the treasure, and concentrate our attention upon it. For the possession of the treasure is the main thing; for one, and for all.

CHRIST, THE GOAL OF SCRIPTURE.

The third thing in our Lord's challenge is the most important of all. It is this, that as the value of the Old Testament is in its revelation of the Way of Salvation, so the Way of Salvation is summed up in Jesus Christ. How true this is, we need only to read the book of Isaiah, in which the Old Testament teaching of eternal life reaches its clearest and completest statement. Salvation there means a personal Savior. The treasure is in the possession of the Messiah, the Suffering Servant of God. There are the clearest intimations of the Incarnation, and of the Atonement, in this great book, which may be said to be the crown of the older Scriptures. And what this book contains, can be traced without difficulty, in psalm, and in sacrifice, and in foreshadowings from the very beginning.

The New Testament presumes the Old. And the Old Testament, without the New, is a broken shaft, a book cut in two. The Old Testament is the dawn, the morning twilight. In the gospels and the epistles, the sun rises above the horizon, and hangs poised in the zenith. Christ is the heart of the Old Testament, as He is the heart of the New. These books, one and all, are but so many massive pillars of granite, and marble, and onyx, and gold, and silver, and burnished brass, forming a magnificent colonnade, converging upon a Throne, in form of a Cross, upon which is seated the Incarnate Son of God, whose scepter of grace welcomes the penitent suppliant. Let us not linger in the porch. Let us advance with swift and eager steps to the inmost shrine of salvation. That is the first thing to do. And having done that, we may examine each column as closely as we choose and can, never forgetting that each is placed where it is, that men may find their way to the world's only and almighty Savior. The Scriptures are the world's guide-book to Jesus Christ; and through Him, to the forgiveness of sins, to the adoption of children, to sanctification, and to the inheritance of eternal glory!

CHAPTER III.

CHRIST AND THE OLD TESTAMENT.

> "And he said unto them, These are the words which I spake unto you, while I was yet with you, that all things must be fulfilled, which were written in the law of Moses, and in the prophets, and in the psalms, concerning me."—LUKE xxiv: 44.

It is not my purpose to conduct a controversial argument. Nor do I propose to enter upon a discussion of purely literary questions, which involve the most delicate and difficult processes, for which my readers have neither time nor taste, and to which no final and universally accepted answer has as yet been given. In fact, my judgment is, that many of these questions never will be answered, unless the sands of the Nile and of the Euphrates shall yield, at the touch of the spade, the buried witnesses of the past. This they have been doing, and most amazing surprises may be in store for us.

THE ILIAD AND THE OLD TESTAMENT.

Many of us are familiar with the Homeric problem. We were told, in our college days, that there never was a Homer: and that the Iliad was not from the pen of any single poet, known or unknown; that it was composite in structure, had been built up by slow accretions, and was legendary throughout. The excavations of Schliemann have reversed all that. The literary critics were blind. The site of Troy has been discovered, and the existence of Homer is conceded.

When Dr. J. P. Thompson visited Berlin in his early manhood, he met the famous Lepsius in the library of the Royal University, and when the young man told the scholar that he hoped at some future time to write a little book on Moses, the German professor exploded: "*But, mein Gott, there never was a Moses!*" That was the fashion fifty years ago. It was assumed that there was no literary activity, and no practise of writing, fifteen hundred years before Christ. That early age was supposed to have been in possession only of knowledge conveyed by oral tradition, which is confessedly insecure and unreliable. But now, the excavations in Assyria, and the discovery of the Tell-Amarna tablets, dug up from the valley of the Nile, prove beyond question, that a hundred years before Abraham, and two thousand years before Christ, there were royal libraries in Egypt, and Babylonia, and Palestine, and that an active correspondence was carried on between these widely separated regions. Moses has come back to stay. Abraham cannot be a myth. They lived in an age of written documents.

THE CRITICISM OF THE NEW TESTAMENT.

Let me briefly touch upon another matter, to show how uncertain are the methods and the results of Biblical criticism. It is said that the Five Books of Moses disclose traces of composite authorship. Very likely; but that goes only a very little way towards determining the number, the date, and the authorship, of the documents. Moses himself may have combined the more important of them. In fact, this was Astruc's theory, who in 1753 led the way in Pentateuchal analysis. He found two documents in Genesis, but claimed that Moses gave them their present shape. The first three gospels present a similar problem. Every one of them is anonymous. Every one of them is composite. They disclose a most remarkable agreement, and no less remarkable differences. Not one of them is a recension of the other two, and not one of them embodies throughout the personal knowledge of the writer. The latter claim can be affirmed only of the Fourth Gospel, which bears a very similar relation to the preceding three, to that which Deuteronomy sustains to the preceding parts of the Pentateuch.

A single sentence from Papias, preserved by Eusebius, the historian, has perplexed students for many years. He says that Mark is supposed to have written down what he heard Peter say about Christ. Is our present Mark the compilation of these notes, or is it a later work, from another hand, based upon these notes? The question cannot be answered. Papias also says that Matthew wrote a gospel in Hebrew. That is still more puzzling. Is our present Matthew a Greek translation of an original and lost Hebrew gospel, or is it a new version by Matthew, or is it from another hand, based upon the original

Hebrew gospel of Matthew, and incorporating material from other sources? The question cannot be answered. Traces of three documentary sources have been found in Matthew and Mark; but the attempts to reproduce them have thus far utterly failed. The third gospel is professedly composite. The writer acknowledges his indebtedness in the preface; and there are traces of two documents in the Book of Acts, one of which is a compilation, while the second is a personal narrative. But this is true of all historical literature. Personal reminiscences are a very small part of it. It sifts and combines the stories of eye-witnesses, and makes free use of earlier written documents; and the more severe and searching the comparison and sifting, the more reliable is the result.

The gospels, then, are composite literature; they could not be anything else; but their historical trustworthiness is beyond successful impeachment. And if the literary questions raised by the evangelistic narratives cannot be definitely answered, it is plain that dogmatism in regard to the Old Testament is out of place. Dr. Philip

Schaff was one of our most learned and catholic American scholars, perfectly at home in German literature; and his ripe judgment may be commended to all who undertake to thread the labyrinth of modern criticism, when he says: "The cause of Biblical criticism has been much injured in the eyes of devout Christians by the hasty and oracular utterances of unproved hypotheses." To criticism, free and fearless, I do not object. It cannot be checked, and it ought not to be checked. But I do protest, in the name of scholarship, against the announcement of doubtful and debatable propositions, as fixed and authoritative criteria in dealing with the Bible. The intolerance of Ewald and Graf is quite as offensive and unbearable, as the tyranny of Hildebrand and Boniface.

HIGHER AND LOWER CRITICISM.

Biblical criticism falls into two general departments. The first, which has come to be known as lower criticism, deals with the text, and attempts, by comparison of manuscripts and versions, to reproduce, as nearly as possible, the original autographs. The second, which has come to be known as higher criticism, deals with the authenticity and the integrity of the books, and endeavors to determine when and by whom they were written, and whether they are independent treatises or drawn from older sources, traditional or documentary. These questions, it is clear, are more difficult and important than the settlement of the text. They are not all of equal importance. An anonymous document may be authentic, unmutilated, and of the highest trustworthiness. A book may be the product of many writers, and reveal unmistakable traces of indebtedness to earlier authorities, mentioned and unmentioned, without detriment to its authority. In fact, such composite structure may increase its credibility. It is more important to know whether the writer had access to trustworthy sources of information, whether he used such sources with impartiality, or whether he was biased, whether the writing in our hands is a forgery, or a mixture of philosophy and fact, or a straightforward narrative conveying its own lessons, and whether the book has come down to us in mutilated or unmutilated form. These questions cannot be entered upon until the text has been settled. Lower criticism must do its work, before higher criticism is equipped for its task.

It is unfortunate that the words "lower" and "higher" have crept into use. Many regard them as invidious, and use them under protest. They are not properly descriptive. It were better if the first department were known as "textual" criticism, which would indicate the exact nature of the task set before it. And the second department should be divided into literary and historical criticism; literary criticism dealing with the analysis of the books, and with the internal evidences indicating their structure, authorship, and time of appearance; historical criticism dealing with the external evidences, supplied by various quotations and references in contemporary literature, inscriptions, monuments, and the like.

THE AUTHORITY OF TRADITION.

It is to be regretted that so many of the Biblical critics are wanting in exact and comprehensive historical knowledge. They look with some disdain upon the students of archæology, and they minimize the established results. But problems of authenticity, and of integrity, cannot be determined by literary analysis alone. The problem is pre-eminently a historical one, and historical evidence alone can solve it. Literary criticism cannot possibly determine by whom a book was written, and if it ventures to cast doubt upon clear and unequivocal statements in the book itself, denying them altogether or reducing them to a minimum, it simply buries us in hopeless bewilderment. Thus it is said that the Pentateuch does not claim to have been written by Moses. But the critics also grant that some things were written by him. And the frequent recurrence of the phrase, "The Lord said unto Moses," which runs like an unbroken thread through the Levitical legislation, could have been warranted only because the tradition assumed authoritative form in his day. To discredit that testimony is to make the problem hopeless of solution. When it is denied that the last twenty-seven chapters of Isaiah are from the pen of that prophet, the fact that the book of Isaiah has always contained them must be allowed to have some weight, and the most positive evidence must be produced, that the natural and inevitable inference of a single authorship is not only unwarranted, but contradicted by the plainest facts. It is a suspicious fact that they who deny the Mosaic authorship of the Pentateuch, and who declare Isaiah to be composite, can do no better than to assign them to some great unknown, and cannot even fix the time when he lived. The result only gives us an indefinite number of Elohists and Jahvists and Deuteronomists and Redactors, shadowy and unsubstantial figures, whose number even cannot be determined. The once famous Fragmentary Hypothesis broke down under the weight of its arbitrary assumptions, and it begins to look as if the present theory would be soon involved in the same fate. The evident unity of the books contradicts the theory of mechanical composite structure. The scissoring and patching become bewildering. At all events, the result leaves us in a hopeless muddle, and when that is the only thing settled, the proposed solution is self-condemned.

It has become the fashion to cast discredit upon tradition. But a traditional solution is better than one which leaves everything hanging in the air, which begins with guesses and ends in fog. The criticism of tradition is legitimate. It may be exaggerated, and it may be false, but whether tradition is exaggerated or false, must be historically determined. Modern criticism simply assumes that tradition is not a competent witness. Its voice is silenced. That is arbitrary, unscientific, and unhistorical. Traditions are rarely, if ever, wholly fictitious and legendary. There is in them a kernel of historical truth, and the more widely traditions have gained currency, the longer they have held their ground, challenged or unchallenged, the more are they entitled to respectful treatment. Thus it is only by tradition that we assign the first three Gospels to the writers with whose names they are associated. Judged simply by their contents, they are anonymous. The traditional account holds its ground for the simple reason that it cannot be discredited by equally good external evidence. So the Pauline Epistles have the Pauline signature stamped upon and into them, and to discredit their Pauline origin demands evidence of the most positive and overwhelming character. It is easy to deny authenticity and integrity, but the denial must be made good. The burden of proof is upon him who denies. He must show that in detail, and as a whole, the traditional view is false. The grounds upon which, for example, the unity of Isaiah is denied, are so shadowy that they cannot be said to nullify the evidence that the book, so far as we know, has never existed in any other than its present form, and has always been attributed to Isaiah. The Pentateuch has always been credited to Moses, and Mosaic authority is stamped upon every one of its parts, while not a particle of external evidence can be produced against the universal tradition. The synagogue is not infallible, but the synagogue from the first regarded Moses as the great author of the Pentateuch, so that from the time of Ezra down this tradition is the only one invested with evidential authority. The tradition will hold its ground, and ought to hold its ground, until the critics do something more than substitute guesses for facts.

THE HISTORICAL TEMPER.

We are assured that no harm can result from the collapse of traditional views. Canon Driver solemnly declares that critical results do not destroy either the authority or the inspiration of the Old Testament. That declaration must be accepted as sincere. Wholesale charges of irreverence and of infidelity do more harm than good. They are not true. No one can read what many of the higher critics have written, without being impressed with their industry, learning, sincerity, and reverence. But it must also be said that in many cases the judicial temper is wanting. They deal in possibilities and probabilities. They approach the problems with a prejudice against the traditional view, and with a depreciatory estimate of historical evidence. They assume that unless the traditional view can be proved, it must be regarded as false, or as at best an unsupported guess. Silence at a certain point is construed as evidence to the contrary. Thus, in many cases there is a break in the testimony, at the year 70, when Jerusalem was destroyed by Titus; and although at that period the tradition is definite and fixed, the absence, beyond that period, of positive evidence is construed as implying ignorance or doubt. But there is no evidence confirming that conclusion; such evidence as there is, is all in favor of the traditional view, so that the critical logic breaks down because it has nothing whatever upon which it rests. The choice must be between a careful sifting of tradition, and agnosticism. Professor Buhl, of Leipzig, shows a most commendable temper of mind when he frankly concedes that the Jews must be regarded "as the authority on the question of the Old Testament canon. The people of Israel, to whom the Old Testament revelation had been entrusted, and whose life task it was to preserve it uncorrupted, are, in fact, the legitimate and competent judges when it has to be decided in what writings this revelation appears in purity and free from all foreign and modifying elements. That we are no longer in a position fully to trace out the principles which led the scribes in their determination regarding the Canon, and that those principles which can still be understood are in many cases extremely peculiar, cannot be regarded, as in this connection, of any importance. For it is not with the views of the scribes that we have to do, but only with the favor shown to the Scriptures and their circulation among the people, of which the decrees of the rabbis as to the Canon are simply an echo. The spread and recognition which the books had won in the genuinely Jewish community is the material which the scribes had to work up in their own way ; but how they succeeded in this is only of secondary interest, while the firm position of the writings among the members of the community affords the special guarantee that they recognized in them a true reflection of their spiritual life, and that these writings, therefore, must be accepted by us as the canonical means of learning to know that life." In the later part of the discussion Professor Buhl declares, that the frequent charges of serious corruption in the text of the Old Testament are absolutely without foundation, and are discredited by the high reverence with which the Scriptures were treated.

It is refreshing to note such a return to the historical temper. Its cultivation must issue in the modification of many current critical judgments, and in the withdrawal of not a few. For while the traditional evidence needs to be historically sifted, it cannot be ignored, especially when it is remembered that all the historical evidence there is, is in favor of the traditional view. And that traditional view, as Buhl states, was not created and imposed by the scribes, but was simply recorded by them as the sifted result of ancient, transmitted, national conviction.

APPEAL TO CHRIST.

There is one fact which remains fixed and historically assured in the bewildering debate, and which is of supreme and decisive importance to the Christian believer. Canon Driver is most emphatic in the statement that the same canon of historical criticism which "authorizes the assumption of tradition in the Old Testament forbids it in the New," and that "the facts of our Lord's life on which the fundamental truths of Christianity depend cannot be anything else than strictly historical." But the New Testament, and even the first three Gospels alone, will give us the present Old Testament, with our Lord's endorsement of it as Scripture. That will be enough for the plain Christian. He will conclude that he cannot do better than to use his Old Testament, as Christ used it, and that he need not hesitate to do so.

CHRIST AND THE OLD TESTAMENT.

The substantial identity, I am prepared to say practically absolute identity, of the present Hebrew Old Testament with the Old Testament as Christ knew it, is one of the clearest outstanding facts in the critical controversy. The debate, for the most part, concerns the period between Ezra, 450 B. C., to Moses, 1491 B. C., a little over a thousand years, whose contemporaneous memorials have perished in the ruthless wars of the captivities, and in the destruction of the temple by the Roman soldiers. But it is equally clear that long before the birth of Christ, the present books of the Old Testament were regarded as Scripture and inspired; were read regularly in the synagogues; were classified as "Law, Prophets, and Psalms," bound up in rolls and jealously guarded, and were studied with a veneration bordering upon superstition. The evidence is ample, massive, and overwhelming. Soon after the destruction of Jerusalem, the learned Jewish rabbis established a colony and organized a famous school at Jamnia, which continued in existence for sixty years; and here, soon after the year 70, the present number and names of the books of the Old Testament were formally and officially promulgated. The list names twenty-four books, and includes every book in our present collection; and it includes only these. The difference between our of thirty-nine books and the Hebrew list, which contains only twenty-four, is accounted for by the fact that in the Hebrew list I. and II. Samuel appear as one book, I. and II. Kings as one book, I. and II. Chronicles as one book, Ezra and Nehemiah as one book and the twelve minor prophets as one book. The difference is purely one of numerical notation; the actual contents are identical.

JOSEPHUS.

Josephus, writing sixty years after Christ's death, about the year 90, gives the number and the classes of the Old Testament books, and speaks of them as long recognized and inspired. The passage has often been quoted and is found in his tract against Apion, the eighth chapter of the first book. The number is spoken of as twenty-two, to make it correspond with the number of the Hebrew alphabet, and this was done by combining Ruth with Judges, and Lamentations with Jeremiah. That the Old Testament of Josephus was identical with our own, is evident from an examination of his "History of the Jews," which draws upon all these books as authoritative sources of historical information. Even Jonah is embodied in the story. The force of the testimony of Josephus will appear, when it is remembered that he was born in the year 37, only seven years after the death of Christ, and that his life covers the lives of the Apostles Paul and John.

The passage is worth inserting: "For we have not an innumerable multitude of books among us, disagreeing from and contradicting each other (as the Greeks have), but only twenty-two books, which contain the records of all past times, which are justly believed to be divine. And of them five belong to Moses, which contain his laws, and the traditions of the origin of mankind until his death. The interval of time was little less than 3,000 years. But as to the time from the death of Moses till the reign of Artaxerxes, King of Persia, who reigned after Xerxes, the prophets, who were after Moses, wrote down what was done in their time in thirteen books. The remaining four books contain hymns to God, and precepts for the conduct of human life. How firmly we have given credit to these books of our own nation is evident by what we do; for during so many ages as have already elapsed no one hath been so bold as either to add anything to them or take anything from them, or to make any change in them; but it is become natural to all Jews, immediately and from their very birth to esteem these books to contain divine doctrines, and to persist in them, and, if occasion be, willingly to die for them. For it is no new thing for our captives, many of them in number, and frequently in time, to be seen to endure racks and death of all kinds upon the theaters, that they may not be obliged to say one word against our laws, or the records that contain them ; whereas there are none at all among the Greeks who would undergo the least harm on that account; no, nor in the case if all the writings that are among them were to be destroyed."

Josephus here speaks for himself and for the nation. He certainly could not be mistaken on that point. He was the most learned and influential Jew of his time, and he was anything but a strict constructionist. It may be that the Bible is a forgery, and it may be that the Declaration of American Independence is forgery ; but the statement of Josephus proves conclusively, that our present Old Testament was regarded in his day with such veneration, that men were prepared to die for their faith in it, and that for many generations before his time it had not been tampered with. The nation, according to his testimony, as early as his own birth in the year 37, accepted the books as we now have them, regarded them as inspired, and affirmed the integrity of the text.

PHILO AND THE SEPTUAGINT.

We can go back fifty years beyond Josephus. Philo, a learned Jew, writing during our Lord's life and immediately after, quotes from nearly every one of our present books, and accords them inspired authority. He quotes from the Pentateuch, Joshua, Judges, Samuel, Kings, Isaiah, Jeremiah, the minor prophets, Psalms, Proverbs, Job, Ezra and Chronicles. We can go back 200 years beyond Philo. He lived and taught at Alexandria. His philosophy was a mixture of Old Testament theology and Greek metaphysics. Alexandria had long been the home of many Jews, who gathered there after the dispersion occasioned by the first destruction of Jerusalem by Nebuchadnezzar, and made the city of their adoption a famous center of Jewish learning and religion. The Jewish colony had at an early day become Greek in speech, and the general neglect of Hebrew had made a Greek translation of the Old Testament necessary. This was begun 280 B. C., and finished about 150 B. C.; accepted and authorative at least 200 years before Philo. Not one of our present books is missing in the

Septuagint, though several others were inserted and added, which went under the name of Apocrypha, and are accepted as canonical and inspired by the Roman Catholic Church, but are rejected by Protestants and Jews. Many of us can remember these books as printed and bound up in our older Bibles, though occupying a separate section.

MEANING OF THE FACTS.

Consider what these facts mean. Add 280 B. C., when the Greek translation was begun, to 1897, and we have 2177. During that long period the Old Testament has been what it is now. It certainly is a modest claim that these books in the Old Testament must have been known, and in general circulation, one or two hundred years before 280 B. C., which brings us to the time of Ezra. In fact, we learn from the Proverbs of Jesus, the son of Sirach, that in the days of his grandfather, 200 years before Christ, the division of the Old Testament into "the Law of Moses, the Prophets, and the Psalms" was already known, and in familiar use; and the use which the author himself makes of these books proves that the first and second parts of this division had precisely the same contents which they have now. The verdict of sober scholarship upon this point, now under consideration, and in which Kuenen, Cornill and Cheyne agree, may be stated in the measured words of Professor Sanday: "The Canon of the Law was practically complete at the time of the promulgation of the Pentateuch by Ezra and Nehemiah, in the year 444 B. C., and that of the prophets in the course of the third century before Christ. As to the closing of the third group, there is perhaps more room for difference of opinion. A common view is that the recognition of these books as Scriptures would be no later than 100 B. C. All the books are quoted as authoritative in recorded sayings from Hillel onward." And Hillel died four years before the Christian era; died in the year in which our Lord was born. This makes it incontrovertibly clear that the Scripture to which Christ appealed is our own Old Testament. That nail should be clinched. The concession of Professor Sanday is all the more impressive, because he grants the documentary structure of the Pentateuch, the post-exilian date of its middle books, locates Deuteronomy in the age of Josiah, places many of the Psalms in the Maccabean time, and maintains the late dates of Ruth and Daniel. But he cannot resist the historical evidence that a hundred years before Christ, the Old Testament as we now have it was universally regarded as inspired Scripture. And when it is remembered how jealously the Jews, 200 years before Christ, guarded their sacred writings, and what superstitious reverence they paid them, what recondite meanings Philo found in names and numbers, we must be permitted to believe, and we cannot resist the positive conviction, that those early students were better equipped to pass judgment upon questions of authorship and date, than are we. Their emphatic and unanimous verdict is at least entitled to respect, even if they were not infallible. Between Ezra and David are only six hundred years, and between Ezra and Moses are only about a thousand years. Between us and David are three thousand years, between us and Moses are thirty-four hundred years, and the period is broken for us by the destruction of Jerusalem under Titus. But in the midst of that tumult stands the Old Testament, in substantially the same form in which we now have it, read in all the synagogues then as it is now, spoken of as Scripture, regarded as inspired, accepted and quoted by Christ as authoritative.

UNCONTRADICTED.

I am not aware that any scholar with competent learning, however critical his attitude, would undertake seriously to call this statement in question. Ewald, Strack, Stanley, Buhl, Delitzsch, Briggs, Robertson Smith, Reuss and Samuel Davidson, concede it. Kuenen and Wellhausen do not challenge it. Even Vernes, who claims that no writing of the Old Testament is of earlier date than Ezra, would not deny it. It is implied upon every page of the New Testament, and the evidence is clear, ample, and decisive, that from the very first the Christian Church accepted in its entirety the Old Testament as it was read and honored in the synagogues and by the nation. The public life of our Lord was one strenuous, unbroken conflict with the Scribes and Pharisees, but He accepted the same Scriptures with themselves as a revelation from God. Paul broke with the synagogue in its theology, but for the ancient oracles he retained his undiminished and unqualified reverence. No criticism can shake that outstanding fact. The temple fell. The holy city crumbled into dust. The priesthood came to an end. Sacrifice ceased. One thing was neither burned nor buried. The Old Testament, as we have it, survived the shock of Roman arms, and, with Christ, it maintained its imperial ascendency, gaining a new and universal constituency. For the notion, advanced by some, that between the first century before Christ and the first century after Christ the Hebrew text was deliberately and seriously corrupted, is utterly without foundation; and the clear testimony of Josephus, who lived in the latter century, falls like a trip-hammer upon those who hint it.

The only plausible qualification which can be made, is that in the time of Christ there was some uncertainty concerning certain books which belong to what is called the third Canon of Scripture. Thus Robertson Smith declares that the Canon of the Law was complete 450 B. C.; the Canon of the prophets 168 B. C., and that in the time of Christ, Psalms, Proverbs and Job were accepted as inspired Scriptures. That would leave out Esther, Ezra and Nehemiah, Ecclesiastes, Canticles, Daniel, and Chronicles. Even these, he declares, were in existence and widely read; only it is claimed that these were not decisively regarded as Scripture until the end of the first century of our era. And here again, the explicit testimony of Josephus falls like a triphammer upon the theory. But even granting it, it is plain that the bulk of our Old Testament was in Christ's hands, and regarded by Him as Scripture. In an Oxford Bible the entire Old Testament covers 585 pages, and these disputed books cover only eighty-nine pages; and their elimination would not alter a single feature in the history down to the time of Ezra. The evidence for our present Old Testament, as endorsed by Jesus Christ, is simply amazing, overwhelming, unanswerable.

THE ARGUMENT DECISIVE.

That settles the controversy for the believer in Christ. There are a hundred questions which it does not answer. But it does clear the ground. It gives us firm footing, and makes the citadel impregnable. The spiritual life of Christ was nourished by these Old Testament Scriptures. To them He appealed as the oracles of God, disclosing to men the way of salvation, and constituting an impressive prophecy of His advent and mission. He appealed to them for nothing else; but in that region He declared them to be authoritative; and among these writings were the five books of Moses, whatever their structure, and the puzzling book of Jonah, be it history or parable, to all of which He referred, and from which He quoted. That is the one thing which is perfectly clear, and that is the one thing to be emphasized, as it is the only thing of vital importance. Christ must be torn out of the heart of the world, before the Old Testament can be wrenched from its place. And in emphasizing what I have, I have turned the entire flank of the critical host, entrenching myself in the impregnable citadel, where the Babel of voices cannot disturb us, and where its cannonade can have no more effect upon us than the shooting of peas against the sun. I simply want to emphasize the fact that if men will use their Old Testament as Jesus Christ used His, which was the same as our own, to find their way to God and heaven, they may go on their way rejoicing, while the critics fight over their endless and profitless task. It is safe to follow Him who gave His life to save us.

OUR LORD'S USE OF THE OLD TESTAMENT.

And how He used them, how He would have us use them, He has Himself told us, in those familiar words with which He defended His august claims, and challenged the Pharisees, words which cannot be considered too often and too seriously: "*Search the Scriptures; for in them ye think ye have eternal life, and they are they which testify of me.*" Here we are told what to search, how to conduct the search, and what the result of a proper search will be. The Scriptures which He commends to us are the Old Testament books in our possession, by which His own life had been nourished and made strong. The temper of our search, in the use of these Scriptures, is to be the earnest endeavor to discover in them the divine message of eternal life. They were given to make us wise unto salvation. And in discharging this peculiar office, they conduct us to Jesus Christ, the beating heart and vital bond of both Testaments.

REFERENCES.

To such as desire to enter upon a more careful and extended study of the problems debated by modern Biblical critics, the following books are commended. The list is only a preliminary one, and could easily be greatly enlarged:

"Moses and His Recent Critics," by Dr. Chambers.
"Moses and the Prophets," by Professor Green.
"The Pentateuch: Its Origin and Structure," by Dr. Bissell.
"The Higher Criticism and the Monuments," by Professor Sayce.
"The Mosaic Origin of the Pentateuchal Codes," by Professor Vos.
"The Foundations of the Bible," by Canon Girdlestone.
"The Early History of Israel," by Professor Robertson.
"The Unity of the Book of Genesis," by Professor Green.
"Supernatural Revelation," by Professor Mead.
"Romans Dissected," by Realsham.
"The Law and the Prophets," by Professor Stanley Leathes.
"Radical Criticism," by Professor Beattie.
"Theological Propadeutic," by Professor Philip Schaff.

"Higher Criticism of the Pentateuch," by Professor Green.

"Genesis and the Semitic Tradition," by Professor Davis.

"Inspiration of the Old Testament," by Principal Cave.

"Book by Book," by Robertson, Davidson, Leathes, etc.

"Canon and Text of the Old Testament," by Professor Buhl, of Leipzig.

"A Study of the Pentateuch," by Professor Stebbins.

"The Bible and Modern Discoveries," by Henry A. Harper.

"The Chaldean Account of Genesis,' by Smith and Sayce.

"History, Prophecy and the Monuments," by Professor McCurdy.

"The Christian View of God and the World," by Professor Orr.

"Patriarchal Palestine," by Professor Sayce.

"The Tell-Amarna Tablets," by Major Conder.

"The Bible, Theocratic Literature," by Principal Simon.

"Christ and Criticism," by Professor Mead.

"The Oracles of God," by Professor Sanday.

"A Layman's Study of the English Bible," by Professor Francis Bowen.

"Nature and Method of Revelation," by Professor Fisher.

"Creation," by Professor Arnold Guyot.

"Modern Skepticism," by Professor Young, of Belfast.

"What is Inspiration?" by Professor De Witt.

"Alleged Discrepancies of the Bible," by John W. Haley.

"Nature and the Bible," by Professor Reusch, of Bonn.

An article of seventy pages in the Presbyterian Review for 1883, by Professor Briggs, may also be consulted with great advantage, though the author at present maintains what less than fourteen years ago he so keenly and mercilessly riddled. There are many, of whom I am one, who think that the learned professor has not succeeded in demolishing his own logic. And a dispassionate survey of the literature on both sides, must lead to the conclusion that nearly the entire territory of modern Biblical criticism is debatable ground, calling for the cultivation of the virtues of modesty and tolerance. Meanwhile, Jesus Christ is in the tossing ship, asleep as it may seem, but with head pillowed upon the Scriptures which we know as the Old Testament!

CHAPTER IV.

CRITICISM AND THE OLD TESTAMENT.

> "The word of God is not bound."
> —TIMOTHY ii.: 9.

"*The word of God is not bound.*" Thank God for that! The assurance comes to us like a strong and steady breeze from the sea on a sultry July day. He who said it spake from a long experience, during which he had encountered the Jew, the Greek, and the Roman, and had convinced and conquered them all. It is matter for profound thanksgiving, that the Scriptures are invested with an authority which is independent of criticism, and which does not require the vindication of scholarship. We do not need to wait until the critics have come to an agreement, before we open our Bibles, and let them instruct and comfort us. But, on the other hand, we may not ignore, nor evade, the duty which God lays upon us to defend the holy oracles, from whatever quarter the attack may come, and however sincere may be the motives which induce it. For one, I can not be silent when I find the faith of many disturbed, and the hearts of many more deeply pained. I would contribute what I may, and as quietly as I can, to the removal of doubt and the confirmation of confidence. Those who are older, I presume, are not disturbed. These things are not new to them. But many who are younger have experienced a somewhat rude awakening, and have wondered what it all means, and to such I feel that I owe a most solemn and sacred duty. I hope I made it clear in the preceding chapter, that no believer in Jesus Christ need hesitate to use the Old Testament, upon which He set the seal of His unmistakable personal endorsement. More, however, needs to be said. Having put my hand to the plow, I must go to the end of the furrow. I proceed to call attention to certain vicious assumptions, which pervade the methods, and determine the results, of the revolutionary criticism of the Old Testament, upon the validity of which any man or woman of ordinary intelligence can pass judgment, and with which technical scholarship has little or nothing to do.

MODERN SCHOLARSHIP.

Let me refer, in passing, and in parenthesis, to the frequent claim that the weight of modern scholarship is with the new school of critics. A good deal depends upon what is meant by weight. The most learned men do not always make the most noise. Newspaper and review notoriety is not always the measure of worth. Some years ago a colored preacher in the South preached a sermon on "De Sun Do Move." It electrified his audience. It secured for him a national reputation. He could have filled the biggest hall in any city, East or West. But he did no damage to the Copernican theory. There was no disturbance in the planetary system. Many will recall another public speaker of great natural gifts, who has entertained large audiences at fifty cents a head, on the "Mistakes of Moses." I never even read the reports of his sayings, but I would have gone a hundred miles on foot to have heard Moses on the mistakes of his critic.

He who startles is always sure of an eager hearing and of a wide audience; the second sober thought comes afterward. And the names which are oftenest seen and heard in present Biblical criticism, by no means represent all the scholarship in Christendom.

Among the most famous theological faculties in Germany, are those of Berlin, Bonn, Breslau, Greifswald, Halle, Königsberg, Leipzig and Tübingen. In these universities there are seventy-three theological professors, of which number thirty belong to the radical school, while forty-three belong to the moderate and conservative ranks. Every one of these men is at home in the literature of his department, and is supposed to be an independent and well equipped scholar. He could not hold his place were he not. The benches would be empty, and he would be starved out. It will be seen from this simple statement that the lines of battle are closely drawn. The so-called liberal wing has increased from ten to thirty during the last twenty-five years, and the conservatives have been reduced from fifty to forty-three; but in the eight great universities which I have named the conservatives still have an actual majority of thirteen; and such a majority at present means a good deal, while it proves conclusively that sweeping claims are not warranted by the facts. Confining attention to the nine great Prussian universities, the radical school is found to be represented by sixteen men, and the conservative school numbers twenty-six, in the older provinces; while in the newer provinces the proportion is eight radicals to nine conservatives; a total of twenty-four radicals, and thirty-five conservatives; a majority of eleven for the conservative party. During the last two years the conservatives have been rapidly gaining on the radicals, and the reaction against radicalism seems to be assuming formidable proportions among the general clergy and laity.

Of the thirty-four books in the list which I have given in the preceding chapter, there are seventeen, just one-half, from the pens of American scholars and specialists, every one of them conservative in tone, every one of them written within the last fifteen years, with full and accurate acquaintance of the most recent literature, and no one can read these books without discovering that these men knew what they were talking about. The statement that scholarship is practically a unit for the radical criticism cannot be made good. It is not true of Europe; it is not true of America. The most prominent advocates of radical criticism among us are Harper, Briggs, Toy, Mitchell, Smith and Haupt. But these men are not the superiors in scholarship of Beecher, Osgood, Green, Mead, Curtiss, Denio and Bissell. Radical criticism is represented in Boston, Yale, Harvard, Cornell, Johns Hopkins, Union, Chicago and Andover. But conservative criticism holds its ground in Bangor, Yale, Hartford, Princeton, Drew, Madison, Auburn, Rochester, Rutgers, Allegheny, Crozer, Lane, Louisville, Chicago, Evanston, Oberlin, Omaha and Oakland. Of Congregational theological seminaries, Andover is the only one which can be classed as radical; Bangor, Hartford, Oberlin and Oakland may be classed as conservative; while Yale and Chicago occupy middle ground, and the mediating critical school is practically conservative. Even Professors Harper, Smith, and Briggs make so many important concessions that they may be regarded as seriously antagonizing the fundamental doctrines of the Wellhausen school, saving their faith in a Divine revelation at the expense of logical consistency. And in the war which is upon us, the lines must be sharply drawn upon the main issues, which are questions of historical criticism, and not niceties of literary analysis. The truth is that the radical critics are still deep in the woods.

THE CRUCIAL QUESTIONS.

At this point it may be well to state what the crucial questions under debate are. When it is said that the majority of critics are agreed in the literary analysis of the Pentateuch, and that the orthodox view is maintained only by a few older scholars, the statement is misleading. The orthodox view is assumed to be that Moses wrote every line in the Pentateuch, including even the account of his death, and that for the matter contained in Genesis he was indebted to supernatural revelations from God. Thus defined, there have been no orthodox Biblical critics for a good many years; if indeed there ever were many. And, in like manner, all scholars who have conceded that Genesis discloses evidences of the use of older documentary and traditional authorities, in narratives, and snatches of poetry, and genealogical tables, and who admit different layers of legislation in the middle books of the Pentateuch, not necessarily committed to writing by Moses; who, for example, grant that Deuteronomy is a separate book, completed in its present form after the death of Moses, that the Priest-code is from a different hand, and that Genesis is a fusion of older documents — have been grouped together. *But this is the very group where the lines of battle are drawn between the radicals and the conservatives.* Orthodoxy has nothing whatever to do with the problem. It is not a question of theology which is under discussion. The phrase orthodox criticism is pure nonsense. One might as well talk of orthodox astronomy or chemistry. The debate lies in the region of hard facts. The criticism concerns *the historical value of the documents which make up our present Pentateuch.* Questions of authorship, of date, and of structure, have become preliminary and subordinate. These very problems are approached with presumptions which cast discredit upon the credibility of the documents, and under whose application the record is reduced to a mass of fables, deliberately invented and forged. At that point, the only proper line of cleavage can be drawn, and when it is drawn there, the radical critics are in a hopeless minority. Sober scholarship repudiates their assumptions, methods and conclusions.

THE CLAIMS OF CRITICISM.

Let me state, as briefly as I can, the claims for which the modern radical criticism is contending. The seriousness of that contention appears only when it is viewed as a whole. Moses, we are told, did not write the Pentateuch. Some things may have been recorded by him, but not very much. The ten commandments, as they appear in Exodus, are certainly not in the form which he gave to them, and the whole story about the giving of the law from Sinai is a poetic invention of much later date, to give impressiveness to the Decalogue. Neither the narratives, nor the laws of the Pentateuch, have in any large and important part come from Moses. The Pentateuch is declared to be, in its main intention, a law book, and its historical material is treated as worthless. The legislation is declared to be the core of the record; and the books, it is claimed, were compiled solely with a view to enforce that legislation. An analysis of these laws is declared to prove that they could not have been enacted until about 450 B. C., at least a thousand years after Moses. They constituted the Priest-code of the second temple, and were for the most part unknown before. But to invest them with the authority of Moses, his name was freely used in the enactments, and the wilderness history of the tabernacle was invented to supply a popular historical coloring. The same thing had been done on a smaller scale two hundred years before Ezra, under the reign of King Josiah, when the Book of the Law was said to have been found in the temple. That Book of the Law is assumed to have been our present Deuteronomy, and when the historian tells us that Hilkiah professed to have *found* Deuteronomy in the temple, we are told that we must interpret this as a very polite hint that the priest had written it himself, in part or entire; in other words, that he had been guilty of a pious literary forgery, in order that, by the help of the authority of Moses, he might wean the people from their idolatry, and concentrate the religious reverence of the nation upon a single central sanctuary. Thus, Deuteronomy is the literary invention of the seventh century B. C., and the Levitical legislation is the literary invention of the fifth century B. C., while in both cases the history is supplied by way of artificial framework. To this latter period also are referred all such narrative materials, as disclose the style and point of view characteristic of the priestly writer; as, for example, the first chapter of Genesis. Then there are supposed to be two other documents, older than either of the preceding, and independent of each other, belonging to the eighth and ninth centuries B. C.; one current in Northern Palestine, the other in Southern Palestine, known as the Elohist and the Jehovist or Jahvist. These four documents are said to have been reduced to their present shape by a Redactor, or by several Redactors, who arranged and altered the materials to suit their purpose. Every document has been tampered with in this way, and the critics do not hesitate to charge the Redactors with both literary awkwardness and dishonesty.

THE CLAIM STARTLING.

This review may startle the reader. It is enough to startle any one who has not lost all faith in the ordinary honesty of the writers of the Bible. But I have not overdrawn the picture. In detail, and as a whole, the history is discredited. Some leave a little truth in the narrative; others leave none at all. Even the reality of the Exodus is denied, and as for the narratives in Genesis, their historical reality is surrendered. The calm verdict of Professor Robertson, of Glasgow, whom the critics claim as one of their number, will commend itself to the cautious and reverent student, when he sums up a long discussion on the Pentateuch in these words: " It may be admitted that the component parts of the books belong to different periods, the death of Moses, for example, being recorded side by side with words spoken and written by Moses. It may be admitted that we have three stages of legislation, as represented in the Book of the Covenant, the Levitical Code, and Deuteronomy; it may be admitted that there are variations in the laws, and an advance from a lower to a higher stage; but all this does not necessitate the assumption that these Codes are separated by intervals of centuries. All this, and much more, may be admitted; but all who would give to the Biblical writers credit for ordinary honesty, will hesitate before admitting that we owe a great part of the Pentateuch to literary fiction. When it is gravely asserted that prophets and the best spirits of the nation framed first one Code, and then another, with the deliberate intention to represent the history of the past as something different from what it actually was, when the so-called historical books have to be expurgated before they can be used as evidence, one may despair of arriving at the truth altogether, or at once set about reconstructing the history without the aid of these books." And Professor Hommel, of Munich, whom the critics also claim, has recently placed himself upon record in these words: "The more I investigate Semitic antiquity, the more I am impressed by the utter baselessness of the view of Wellhausen."

THE PENTATEUCH A NARRATIVE.

We have noticed that the critics assume that the Pentateuch is primarily a book of laws, and that the history is subordinate to the legislation. Let us read now the Pentateuch for ourselves, and we shall discover that the very reverse is true. From cover to cover the five books of Moses deal with history, and the laws are inserted only as part of the history. The historic thread is renewed in Joshua, carried on through Judges, and pursued through the books of Samuel and Kings. One plain, practical purpose controls the entire literature—to trace the fortunes of Israel from the call of Abraham to the captivity, and the chapters of Genesis preceding the call of Abraham furnish the historical preface to his separation. Narrative is the primary and pervading element. In the New Testament, the legal portions are regarded as having been set aside and annulled, but the history is regarded and referred to as authentic. Be the author or authors of the Pentateuch who they may be, the critics blunder in assuming that they concentrated their attention upon the legal enactments. These are woven into the history at the points where they belong, and then the history proceeds without reference to them. It was the story upon which their interest was centered, and this must determine our critical handling of the history which they have given us. It is an arbitrary, unwarranted, and criminal method of procedure, to discredit their honesty and veracity in the very field where they have concentrated and massed their abilities and resources.

Passing, now, this arbitrary and mischievous reversal of critical perspective, let me ask attention to certain other equally unfounded assumptions, upon which the new critics build their revolutionary conclusions.

THEORY OF EVOLUTION.

One of these assumptions, to which great and decisive prominence has recently been given, is that the so-called theory of evolution has been scientifically established, and should therefore be accepted as a canon of criticism. It has been invested with the authority of the multiplication table; so that whatever does not square with it must be false, so false that we need not trouble ourselves about it. The theory is assumed to be the one supreme law in the realms of matter and of mind. It shapes history, and gives birth to religion, just as it molds the stars. All things begin at the lowest point conceivable, and thence, by gradual stages, they advance to an ever-enlarging perfection. There are no breaks in the process. There are no gaps in the march. There are no interventions, no miracles, and hence all miraculous accounts are scientifically absurd. Man has come up from the sea-slime, and has been constantly rising. Sin is only the remnant in him of his animal ancestry A fall from primitive innocence there never has been, and the first chapters of Genesis are purely fabulous—exquisite poetry, but historically false. Evolution is the infallible touchstone by which the Bible and Christianity must stand or fall.

But the principle is not logically carried out. For there are many who, while they boldly cut out all miracles from the Old Testament, dare not use the surgery upon the New. They claim that the high theology of Deuteronomy and of the Psalms proves these books to be a late literary product; but they dare not assert this of the Gospels and the Epistles of the New Testament. They claim that the primitive Mosaic religion must have been very crude, but they dare not say that about apostolic Christianity. They claim that from Moses to Ezra there was an uninterrupted advance; they dare not say that of the history between Paul and Luther. They minimize the miracles of the Exodus, and of Daniel in the den of lions, but they grant that Christ was born of a virgin and that He rose from the dead. Let us have thorough work. And thorough work demands that with the elimination of the miraculous and supernatural in the Old Testament, the same elements shall be cut out of the New. Moses and Christ, the Law and the Gospel, fall into the same grave. And the only reason why this is not done in the case of Christ

CRITICISM AND THE OLD TESTAMENT. 113

and the Gospel, is because the facts of Christianity are so stubborn that the critics do not venture to beat their heads against them. They prefer to be inconsistent, rather than stultify themselves. But that very hesitancy shows the inherent weakness of the claim.

WHAT IS EVOLUTION?

What, now, is evolution? Darwin and Wallace did not agree in their definition, and in the scope of its application. Wallace insisted that it did not apply to man. The word has never yet been defined.

Everybody uses the word, and presumably knows its meaning; yet nobody seems to be able to give a definition which is clear and final. No magician's wand can play so many fantastic tricks as can this word. It can be theistic and atheistic, to suit the speaker's taste. It can eliminate miracles, and it can make them feel at home. At one time it bows God out of the universe, and has no use for Him; at another time it makes him immanent, omnipresent and omnipotent, enthroned and personally active in every atom. Renan needed no God to account for the origin of things. But his theory of evolution provided for the ultimate appearance of a man who would master the secret of death and life, and who would thus empty all the graveyards of the past, bestowing immortality upon every one of their hapless victims. So that evolution can give birth even to God. There is no God at the beginning, but there is one at the end. It is plain, therefore, that evolution may be so defined as to provide for supernatural intervention and guidance, and for the most astounding miracles. But the trouble is that these stay only in the definition. Practically they are excluded, and what remains may be summed up in the following items:

1. The affirmation that the higher grades of being have proceeded from the lower by natural generation, and that all grades of being have a common, natural ancestry. The fire-mist has given birth to crystals and to genius, to coral reefs and to the Christian religion.

2. The affirmation that this unfolding has been unbroken and continuous, without a single gap and without creative epochs.

3. The affirmation that the result has been reached by the operation of inherent forces, neither requiring nor permitting the superintendence and the guidance of the personal God. The universe is self-evolved, and self-evolved from the primitive atom. This is what evolution is made to mean by its great advocates, whether they so define it or not. It makes the polyp the real ancestor of man, and eliminates the supernatural from science, literature and history.

NOT ESTABLISHED BY SCIENCE.

The common element in all definitions, which are radical, is the denial of creative epochs, the affirmation that the complexity of the universe, man included, has been the result, in unbroken progression, under natural law, by inherent forces, of rudimentary cells and atoms. The universe has grown out of the atom, as the oak grows out of the acorn. There is difference in the result, but there is identity of method. Now, if anything is clear, it is perfectly clear that this amazing theory has not been made out. There are several gaps which have never been bridged.

The universe is supposed to have had its origin in a sea of raging fire, whirling with inconceivable rapidity, gradually cooling and condensing, throwing off rings now and then, and so forming suns and stars. If that fire-mist ever contained any living germs, they must have been utterly destroyed long before the planets cooled. Whence, then, came life? It is here; how did it emerge from that furnace of fire? We are told that the cell evoluted from the atom. We are asked to believe in spontaneous generation. Huxley believed that, but he also very frankly admitted that all the scientific evidence of two hundred years was squarely against him, and that there was no known exception to the old dictum: "*Omne vivum ex vivo*"—*all life from life*. The atoms refuse to give birth to a cell; and at that point evolution breaks down. It breaks down again when we pass from plants to animals. The cells look exactly alike under the microscope, and we could not tell which belonged to a maple and which to an elephant, but the vegetable cell refuses to give birth to the animal cell. Break number two. Evolution breaks down again when we try to pass from the animal to man. Self-inspection and self-judgment, the activity of the higher reason and of conscience, the seeds of these are not in the brute. Break number three. These tremendous gaps condemn the theory. Intermediate forms are wanting between the inorganic and the organic, between plants and animals, between animals and man. At these points the transition is sharp and sudden, so that even Mr. Huxley protested against the maxim, "*Natura non facit saltum*," and insisted that nature did make leaps. But an evolution which must be helped out by leaps, admits just what the creation theory affirms, and admits all which it affirms. Such an evolution is in exact agreement with the first chapters of Genesis, which affirm that even man was made from the dust of the ground, but not through the operation of forces inherent in plant and animal forms of life. I have mentioned only three gaps. The great German scientist, Du Bois-Reymond, pointed out seven "impassable chasms." And Virchow designates the radical evolutionists as "bubble companies." The facts prove that while there is truth in evolution, the development has its fixed limitations, and identity of descent for all living forms is emphatically negatived. At all events, it is a pure assumption. In evolution, as an orderly development and advance, every intelligent man believes ; and in that sense the doctrine is as old in literature as the first chapter of Genesis. But evolution, as a process of uninterrupted differentiation of being, under natural laws, and from inherent forces, is an unproved theory, with all the evidence squarely against it. So long as that is true, I, for one, am not going to let evolution reconstruct my Bible for me.

FALSE IN LITERATURE AND HISTORY.

I claim more. I claim that while, in the realm of science, evolution is an unproved theory, in the realms of literature and history it is demonstrably false. It is not true that the earliest literature of a nation is the crudest, and its latest the best. It is not true that the line is one of steady improvement. This is not true of Greece, or Rome, or Germany, or France, or England, or the United States. Homer never had a competitor. Shakespeare and Milton have not yet been eclipsed. Socrates, Plato, and Aristotle are still unrivaled. Madison and Jefferson were not pigmies compared to our present statesmen. Washington is still without a peer. We are not more skillful builders than the men who reared the pyramids, nor are we greater architects than the men who designed and superintended the cathedrals. We have not eclipsed the old masters in painting, sculpture, and music. Civilizations do not necessarily grow better as they grow older. Turkey, India, and China prove the very reverse. They have been rapidly going down. A book on "Degeneration" a few years ago attracted wide attention. The picture was overdrawn. But the fact is that it requires the strenuous and continuous exertions of all good men to prevent things from becoming hopelessly bad. The machines are everywhere and always against righteousness and improvement. Progress is not due to them, but to the men who break away from them.

PERSONALITY.

There is one force in literature and in history of which evolution takes no account, and which it cannot explain. It is personality; strong, self-poised, determined personality. Again and again, a man appears who challenges the world to combat, and he wins. It may be Paul; it may be Athanasius; it may be Luther; it may be Jesus Christ. Such men are prophets of God, and they inaugurate new epochs. They shatter prisons and set men free. They arrest the growing degeneracy and usher in the better days. They are not the product of blind and inherent evolutionary forces. One, at least, has defied every attempt at classification. He stands alone, unapproached and unapproachable — the Son of Mary, the Carpenter of Nazareth, the Prophet of Galilee. Nothing in Greece, or Rome, or Judea, explains Him. He was and remains the absolute antithesis of His time, and of all times. Evolution goes to pieces when it touches Him. God is manifest when He appears. And what is true of Christ, is true of every great leader who has appeared in history. Personality dominates in literature, in art, in history, in war and in peace. Carlyle may have gone too far in his hero worship, in his unstinted praise of great and energetic men. There is moral force, for good or evil, in the people, too; and we neglect that at our peril. Still it remains true that personality is the decisive force in history. And personality is the absolute antithesis of evolution. Unproved in science, demonstrably false in literature, art and history, the theory of evolution cannot be accepted as a canon of criticism. Certainly, not at its demand, shall I cease to believe and preach that God created man in His own likeness and image, that man fell by voluntary transgression, and that Jesus Christ was born of a virgin, died to save man, and rose again from the sepulcher.

THE QUESTION OF DATE.

I have dealt with the most formidable assumptions first, when perhaps I should have considered them last. A third assumption upon which the new critics proceed, is that by literary analysis and dissection they can fix the date of a writing, and determine its authorship, without reference to tradition and in direct opposition to it. But the first of these can be done only by comparison with contemporaneous literature. We know, for example, the style and the spelling of Chaucer's time. If now an anonymous manuscript, without date, should be discovered, written in that ancient style, and found in every respect to correspond to it, we could locate the time of its composition. And if such a writing should claim to have been written in that early time, and should, upon comparison, be found to employ the style current five hundred years later, we should pronounce it a forgery. The method is legitimate, but there must be contemporaneous literature. The new critics argue from the style of the Old Testament books to the date of their first appearance; but they argue in a circle, because there is no contemporaneous literature. The Old Testament is the only Hebrew literature which has come down to us from the centuries before Christ. It is impossible to determine by literary analysis what is oldest and what is newest. And, in fact, the critics are using this argument from style with less and less frequency and confidence. Vernes insists that the argument from style is absolutely worthless.

THE PROBLEM OF AUTHORSHIP.

The discovery of authorship by literary dissection is still more difficult. Let me give an illustration. A hundred and twenty-five years ago the letters of Junius created intense excitement in England. They were a sharp and severe arraignment of public men. The author did not hesitate to attack the crown. Everybody tried to find out who he was, and from his retirement he defied them all. He was evidently a man of great ability, and acquainted with State secrets. Men winced under his saber strokes. Had he been discovered it would have fared badly with him. Every art of literary criticism has been used in the attempt to extract the secret. But the secret died with the author and one or two of his friends, and it never will be known who Junius was. This shows the impotence of literary analysis. If a book is anonymous, no literary dissection, in the absence of historical evidence or ancient tradition, can solve the problem. It must be credited to some unknown man, and that leaves us no wiser than before. If the critics cannot tell us who wrote the Pentateuch, they do not help us much. If they cannot locate the documents, they do not help us much. Their guesses do not make us wiser. If they cannot tell us who wrote the last twenty-seven chapters of Isaiah, they do not help us much. Ewald says there were seven of them, but he cannot name one of them. He does not help us much. Meanwhile, the Pentateuch is one unbroken narrative, in the course of which some things are positively declared to have been committed to writing by Moses, while all of it is said to have been commanded or authorized by him; so that it looks as if he had more to do with it, than all the Elohists and Jahvists and Deuteronomists and Redactors combined. Meanwhile, the last twenty-seven chapters of Isaiah have always been bound up in the same book with the preceding chapters, and are found to have been attributed to him as early as two hundred years before Christ; so that the authorship of Isaiah remains as firm as ever, in spite of all the critics have said. The literary analysis of assumed anonymous documents is, and must always be, absolutely fruitless, and it has added nothing to our knowledge. It has provoked our admiration for its patience and brilliancy; it has supplied us with any number of ingenious guesses; but it has not enlightened our darkness with so much as one flash of light.

RUTH AND CANTICLES.

The arbitrariness of the critical procedure, and the barrenness of its results, may be illustrated from two examples — the way in which the books of Ruth and Canticles are handled. Ruth is by many critics located at the period of the Exile. Wellhausen places it considerably later, after Chronicles, because he claims that the genealogical paragraph with which Ruth ends must have been borrowed from Chronicles. Canon Driver says this paragraph may have been added by a later hand, and claims that the purity of the style points to an early date. In the case of Job, however, no weight is given to this argument. In Ruth it is decisive, in Job it is worthless. Davidson credits Ruth to the age of Hezekiah. Robertson Smith says the language is post classical; Driver says it is classical. Neither knows anything about it.

The Song of Solomon supplies an even more impressive illustration of the barrenness of critical handling. The inscription is part of the text, and in the most unqualified way affirms the Solomonic authorship. It is declared to be his "Song of Songs"—that is, the choicest of his songs. It has never been credited to any one else. The tradition is ancient and uniform. In the second century before Christ, the Book of Ecclesiasticus credits it to Solomon. Of course, the critics deny that Solomon had anything to do with it. But not one of them can tell us who was the author, nor when and where he lived. They tell us that these things are involved in obscurity. Some have argued for a late date, from the style. Others have shown most conclusively that there is no such degeneracy, and that the peculiarities in the diction are nothing more than poetical abbreviations, or variations belonging to the Hebrew dialect of Northern Palestine, where we know that Solomon had a magnificent summer palace; so that the majority of those who deny that Solomon composed Canticles, place the poem within a decade or two after Solomon's death, and make it anonymous. This is the judgment of Davidson, Smith, and Driver. And there is nothing harsh in saying, that such a conclusion is simply a confession that the critics do not know what to do with the book. Their concessions are so material, that the Solomonic authorship is the simplest solution, but this they deny by simply saying that he could not possibly have written it. And this is a fair sample of a good deal of higher criticism.

THE CRITICAL PARTITION.

Let me add another example, showing the arbitrariness and the barrenness of the critical procedure. It is almost incredible in what bewildering mazes the literary critics lose themselves, in attempting to trace the lines of composite structure. Genesis is the easiest book by which to pass judgment upon the soundness of their methods. With it Astruc began, and its literary analysis has been conducted with painstaking care. In their views of Genesis, too, the critics are more generally agreed than they are at any other point. Genesis is supposed to represent the work of not less than seven men, reduced to its present form by the Redactor. Of course, these men are unknown, and they are designated P, J, J¹, E, JE, R, and one who is not named, whom we may call X. A cursory examination of Genesis shows that the Redactor is supposed to have embodied 65 paragraphs from P, 137 paragraphs from J, 90 paragraphs from E, 5 paragraphs from J¹, 6 paragraphs from JE, one entire chapter from X, and that 105 paragraphs have been inserted by himself, to say nothing of twenty glosses. This makes 409 pieces in a book covering thirty-seven pages in an Oxford Bible; and these pieces vary all the way from a single word and half a line, to paragraphs and entire chapters. The result may be judged by analyzing the story of Joseph, as given in the thirty-seventh chapter. It contains 127 lines. The critics assign it to five different hands, and they distribute the parts as follows, beginning with the first line:

Three lines from P, 3 lines from JE, 2½ lines gloss, 1½ lines from E, 7 lines from J, 1½ lines from E, 1 line from R, 9 lines from E, 2 lines from R, 4½ lines from E, 1 line from R, 6½ lines from E, 23 lines from JE, 6 lines from E, 1 word from R, 2 lines from J, 5 lines from E, 2½ lines from JE, 1 line from J, 3½ lines from JE, 1 line from J, 3½ lines from JE, 11 lines from J, 2 lines from E, 2 lines from J, 8½ lines from E, 6½ lines from J, 3 lines from E, 5 lines from J, 2½ lines from E.

Was there ever such a literary patch quilt? Thirty pieces dovetailed together in a chapter of thirty-six verses, and in a story which constitutes a plain continuous narrative? The miracle of Jonah and the fish sinks into insignificance before such a literary performance. "*Credat Judæus Apella!*" which being interpreted means "*Tell it to the marines!*"

The critics contend that the sixth, seventh, eighth, and ninth chapters of Genesis contain two originally separate and independent versions of the flood, and in the analysis they claim to have reached substantial unanimity. Four authors have been detected—J¹, J, P and R—whose work appears in 42 pieces. In this section of Genesis there are 328 lines, and they are distributed as follows:

Fifteen and one-half lines from J¹, 8½ lines from J, 1½ lines from R, 2½ lines from J, 46 lines from P, 8½ lines from J, 3 words from R, 6½ lines from J, 2 lines from P, 6½ lines from J, 6 words from R, 5 words from J, 3 words from R, 1 word from J, 1 word from R, 3 lines from J, 5½ lines from P, 2 lines from J, 14 lines from P, 6 words from J, 4 words from P, 2 words from R, 3 words from P, 2 lines from J, 13 lines from P, 4½ lines from J, 3 lines from R, 2 lines from J, 8½ lines from P, 2½ lines from J, 8½ lines from P, 2½ lines from J, 8½ lines from P, 22 lines from J, 3½ lines from P, 2½ lines from J, 18 lines from P, 13½ lines from J, 56 lines from P, 6 lines from R, 4 lines from J¹, 3 words from R, 20 lines from J¹, 4 lines from P.

Now it may be that the mysterious Redactor used his scissors and pot of paste in this most ingenious and amazing fashion; but honestly, I don't believe one word of it.

At whatever point the examination is made, the result is the same. Single sentences are distributed among two and three writers, combined by the Redactor, and paragraphs are broken into fragments. Thus, in the account of the plagues, recorded in Exodus viii: 8—xi: 10, covering 440 lines, the critical partition of Wellhausen yields the following result:

22 lines from P, 15 lines from J, 4 lines from E, 4 lines from J, 11 lines from P, 17 lines from E, 9 lines from P, 3 lines from E, 18 lines from J, 11 lines from P, 29 lines from J, 20 lines from P, 36 lines from J, 15 lines from E, 34 lines from J, 35 lines from E, 52 lines from J, 10 lines from E, 2 lines from J, 3 lines from E, 2 lines from J, 7 lines from E, 14 lines from J, 29 lines from E, 6 lines from J, 15 lines from E, 23 lines from J.

This makes 27 pieces, varying all the way from 2 lines to 52 lines, dovetailed together by the Redactor. Dillmann makes no less than 52 pieces, and Jülicher detects 50; while both add one to the number of the contributors to whom Wellhausen assigns the accounts; Wellhausen being content with three, while Jülicher and Dillmann require four. Thus vanishes the boasted unanimity of the critics, when they come to apply their principles of literary partition.

Even if we confine attention to the first and second chapters of Genesis, from which Astruc drew the hypothesis of two documents, the improbability of the theory seems to me apparent. Here the first chapter is assigned without a break to P, who is now located at the time of the Exile, though until twenty-five years ago this chapter was assigned to the Elohist, who was regarded as the oldest of the writers. The hand of P is traced into the second chapter, as far as the middle of the fourth verse, when the narrative of J is supposed to begin, and to continue through the remaining part of the chapter. Not uninterruptedly, however. There is a break at the tenth verse, when the Redactor inserts five verses, or $13\frac{1}{2}$ lines. Nor is that all. The Redactor has amended J in thirteen places, by inserting the word *God* after the word *Lord*, for the phrase is "*the Lord God*," which, according to the present theory, the Jahvist could not have written. He wrote only *Lord* or *Jehovah*, and *Elohim* or *God* was added by the Redactor, to whom the latter word was more familiar, as Jehovah in his day was no longer in ordinary use. He might quite as easily have erased *Lord* and substituted *God* while he was taking liberties with his text, but had he done so the critics would have been compelled to assign the second chapter to the same writer as the first; and it may be that in this he was unconsciously guided by divine inspiration, in order that the literary critics of the nineteenth century might have the opportunity to exercise and exhibit their penetration!

THEISTIC EVOLUTION.

We are asked to believe in a theistic evolution, in which God permits the race, through nearly three thousand years, to regard as a true and authentic record what he finally enables men to see is a mass of fables, forgeries, and deliberate inventions. For myself, I could not trust in a God who made use of such a method of revelation. It may be all true, what the critics say; but honestly, I don't believe a word of all this rubbish. On the face of it, it is simply incredible that Genesis was put together as the critics claim. I believe in free discussion. But I also protest against what Professor Sayce has well called the papacy of the modern critical school. We are browbeaten by being told that the consensus of scholarship has settled this matter. I deny that there is such consensus, and if there were, it would not be the first time that truth has been in the minority. I call for the facts. I do not care for names. What is needed is a good deal more of quiet, independent investigation, and a good deal less of toadying to a few reckless leaders. I can only say for myself, that the oftener I have reviewed the facts and the logic, and the more carefully I have sifted the evidence, the more convinced I become that the old fable of the mountain and the mouse is repeating itself in the herculean labors of modern criticism.

NON-OBSERVANCE OF A LAW.

I will refer to only one more critical assumption, which must be sharply challenged. It is that the non-observance of a law is evidence of its ignorance by the people, and of its non-existence. The historical books, we are told, show that there was no central and exclusive sanctuary, but that sacrifices were freely and frequently offered in many places. Deuteronomy and the Levitical Code plainly forbid this. Therefore, it is argued, Exodus, Leviticus, Numbers and Deuteronomy could not have been written until many centuries after Moses. Of course, the testimony of Chronicles is thrown out of court, on the ground that it is a late compilation. The major premise of the argument is, that general violation of a law proves its non-existence. I asked a prominent lawyer of my acquaintance, what he thought of that logic. "Why," he answered, "that is unmitigated nonsense." For, as he intimated, there might be such a conspiracy against law, on the part of public officials and judges, as to make it a dead letter, and in a generation the statute might not be so much as referred to or quoted.

Some time after this conversation, I came across a quotation from Sir J. Stephen's lectures on the "History of France," to which Professor Zenos, of Chicago, had called the attention of Professor Green, of Princeton, singularly confirming this judgment by the actual oblivion of an entire code of laws. The quotation is as follows: "When the barbarism of the domestic government (under the Carlovingian dynasty) had thus succeeded the barbarism of the government of the State, one of the most remarkable results of that political change was the disappearance of the laws and institutions by which Charlemagne had endeavored to elevate and civilize his subjects. Before the close of the century in which he died the whole body of his laws had fallen into utter disuse throughout the whole extent of his Gallic dominions. They who have studied the charters, laws and chronicles of the later Carlovingian princes most diligently, are unanimous in declaring that they indicate either an absolute ignorance or an entire forgetfulness of the legislation of Charlemagne."

If this actually happened after the death of

Charlemagne, why was it impossible after the death of Moses? Now, the record shows that this is just what did take place in the centuries after Moses. The history constantly affirms that Israel was unfaithful, and that sacrifice on the high places was an unauthorized innovation. But rulers and priests encouraged it, and the old law fell into disuse and oblivion, until in the reformation under Josiah the authority of the neglected and forgotten law was reinstated. That is a perfectly simple and straightforward account. Hilkiah's discovery of the roll of the law was an event like Luther's dragging the New Testament to light. Even priests had ceased to read it, and the people knew nothing of its contents. If we are to conclude that the non-observance of a law is evidence of its non-existence, then we must conclude that the Ten Commandments and the Sermon on the Mount are not in existence now. The truth is that the historical and prophetic books constantly assume that the Israelites were flagrantly disobedient, and were sorely punished for their disobedience. They had the law, but they kept it not, and the priests were at the feet of the wicked kings. Israel had its dark ages, as the Christian Church has had. In Josiah's time came the great reformation and return, for which the great prophets had prepared the way; and, after the Babylonian captivity, with its humiliating and painful experiences, Ezra and his associates gave to the reformation and return their final and permanent form. The next step was the advent of Jesus Christ. In Him the old passed forever away, and the new appeared upon the scene. With Him we begin. And in His hands we find the same Old Testament, in which He assures us that the way of eternal life is clearly revealed, and of which He exhorts us to make diligent use. From its ceremonial penances and sacrifices He has delivered us, by the sacrifice of Himself upon the Cross. He has abolished the law of ordinances. From the yoke of a human priesthood He has freed us, because He is the eternal High Priest of our glorious redemption. But there remain the record of God's dealings with the men of ancient times, and the psalms of the ancient Church, and the stirring prophecies of bygone centuries, which, as Isaac Taylor has said, have been the drum-beat to which modern progress marches. They are old, but they are not antiquated. They are granaries of bread and wells of salvation. Let us eat and drink, and give thanks to God for His royal bounty.

REVELATION BY DEEDS.

Not words, but deeds, constitute the most impressive revelation of God. He speaks to men through history. He came by Jesus Christ. And the Incarnation was only the crown of an unbroken historic revelation. Not in legal codes and in ritual ordinances are we to search for the secret and vital principle of God's self-revelation, but in the historical events in which they are imbedded, and which make them radiant with eternal meaning. The codes do not touch our life. We may ignore them. The history which underlies and overlaps the codes, has not spent its force. We cannot ignore it. We cannot afford to lose it. The whole patriarchal history, and the discipline of Israel, are luminous with warning and encouragement. We are enriched by the narratives of Abraham, and Joseph, and Moses, and Joshua, and the Judges, and the Kings, loyal and rebellious. There are no better stories for our children. There are no more impressive narratives for the oldest. They constitute an invaluable primer of morality and religion. They were written and preserved for our admonition. They are not cunningly devised fables. And simply in the interest of fair treatment, we protest against their wholesale slaughter upon such wild assumptions as have been passed under rapid review.

FREE DISCUSSION.

It has become the fashion, in critical quarters, to sneer at Professor Green, of Princeton. It will do him no harm. He certainly has no disposition to padlock free thought and free speech. It is only a fool who sits down on the safety valve. Professor Green is on record as saying that "every attempt to interfere with freedom of inquiry on this subject should be frowned down from whatever quarter it may proceed or by whatever object it may be actuated—and vigorous threshing will free the pure grain from the worthless chaff." If that be uncharitable narrowness, then I want my name added to the list of its victims. If men will persist in emptying their wagon loads of criticism upon the public threshing floor, I shall not denounce them, nor will I run away in holy horror, but I will seize my flail and beat away until straw and grain fly apart in clouds of whirling dust. That is true charity. That I understand to be the demand of Christian friendship. And the fearless attitude of Professor Green, to which I have alluded, recalls a similar manly challenge from the lips of the late Dr. Van Dyke, of Brooklyn, most conservative of theologians, when, shortly before his death, his voice rang out in this magnificent fashion: "If we must choose between orthodoxy and liberty, we will hold fast to liberty and let orthodoxy go!" That was said when the critical debate was convulsing the Presbyterian Church. It startled not a few. I thought that I understood him, and I did. I interpreted him as meaning that orthodoxy had nothing to fear from the freest and the most searching discussion, that liberty was the mother of orthodoxy and its perpetual safety. And when I wrote him, asking whether I had caught his meaning, back came the reply by the very next mail, "That is exactly what I had in mind, and what I believe."

Nobody will be privately or publicly admonished to keep still. Congregationalism, at least, has no use for such ecclesiastical machinery. Nobody will be denounced for saying what he believes. But every man will be held responsible for his utterances, and if these utterances defy both fact and logic, the exposure will be made without recourse to apology. In all this there is no bitterness, as there is no persecution. It is simply the protest of manly, intelligent conviction. The critics must expect vigorous handling. Free speech is not their monopoly. It is the divine birthright of every man. Truth has no personal controversy with any man. But arbitrary assumptions, and imaginary facts, and vicious methods, and wholesale charges of fraudulent handling, which, as we have seen, are common with the advocates of radical and revolutionary criticism, cannot be permitted to go unchallenged, and in such a debate plain speech is the best. I have not said a tithe of what might be said.

But I have said enough to prove my main contention true, that the new critics have utterly failed to make out their case, and that to surrender to them at this juncture would be the height of criminal cowardice.

When, thirty years ago, I entered the ministry, the crisis of the destructive criticism on the New Testament had only just passed. We were in the restless waters produced by the exhaustion of a terrific storm, and that, as some of us know, is worse than the tempest. The cyclone was over, but it had cut a terrible swath, and the desolation seemed hopeless. I have lived to see the school of Baur and Renan buried out of sight, and the New Testament intrenched more strongly than ever. The school of Wellhausen is only nineteen years old. If I live twenty years longer, I shall expect to see it laid out for solitary burial, with none to mourn over its departure. The archæologists are already in open revolt. Recent publications in Holland and Germany show that scholarship refuses to be silenced by clamor. The threshing will go on, and it needs no prophet's eye to see that the revolutionary principles upon which the destructive criticism has been conducted, will be thoroughly discredited, and the house built upon the sand will collapse. Meanwhile, in perfect serenity of mind, let us follow Jesus Christ, who grew in favor with God and man, through reverent familiarity with the Scriptures of the Old Testament!

NOAH WEBSTER AND THE BIBLE.

In this connection, and as a fitting ending to what has been said, let me insert a paragraph from the introduction to Webster's Dictionary, written in 1847, four years after his death. Even as early as his day, educated men were acquainted with the criticisms calling in question the integrity and inspiration of the Scriptures. Ewald was his contemporary. German criticism had eager and enthusiastic disciples in New England. Theodore Parker had popularized its doctrines in the early part of the present century. Noah Webster lived in a university town, where Timothy Dwight in his own day was doing valiant service in behalf of evangelical religion. The account proceeds as follows: "In respect of religion Dr. Webster was a firm believer during a large part of his life in the great distinctive doctrines of our Puritan ancestors, whose character he always regarded with the highest veneration. There was a period, however, from the time of his leaving college to the age of forty, that is, between 1778 and 1798, when he had doubts as to some of those doctrines, and rested in a different system. Soon after he graduated, being uncertain what business to attempt, or by what means he could obtain subsistence, he felt his mind greatly perplexed and almost overwhelmed with gloomy apprehensions. In this state, as he afterwards informed a friend, he read Johnson's 'Rambler' with unusual interest, and in closing the last volume, he made a firm resolution to pursue a course of virtue through life, and to perform every moral and social duty with scrupulous exactness. To this he added a settled belief in the inspiration of the Scriptures and the governing providence of God, connected with highly reverential views of the divine character and perfections. Here he rested, placing his chief reliance for salvation on a faithful discharge of all the relative duties of life, though not to the entire exclusion of dependence on the merits of the Redeemer. In this state of mind he remained, though with some misgiving and frequent fluctuations of feelings, to the winter of 1807-8. At that time there was a season of general revival interest at New Haven, under the ministry of Rev. Moses Stuart. To this Dr. Webster's attention was first directed by observing an unusual degree of tenderness and solemnity of feeling in all the adult members of his family. He was thus led to reconsider his former views, and inquire, with an earnestness which he had never felt before, into the nature of personal religion, and the true ground of man's acceptance with God. He had now to decide not for himself only, but, to a certain extent, for others, whose spiritual interests were committed to his charge. Under a sense of this responsibility he took up the study of the Bible with painful solicitude. As he advanced, the objections which he had formerly entertained against the humbling doctrines of the Gospel were wholly removed. He felt their truth in his own experience. He felt that salvation *must* be wholly of grace. He felt constrained, as he afterwards told a friend, to cast himself down before God, confess his sins, implore pardon through the merits of the Redeemer, and then to make his vows of entire obedience and devotion to the service of his Maker. With his characteristic promptitude he instantly made known to his family the feelings which he entertained. He called them together the next morning, and told them, with deep emotion, that, while he had aimed at the faithful discharge of all his duties as their parent and head, he had neglected one of the most important — that of family prayer. After reading the Scriptures, he led them, with deep solemnity, to the throne of grace, and from that time continued the practise, with the liveliest interest, to the period of his death. He made a public profession of religion in April, 1808. His two oldest daughters united with him in the act, and another, only twelve years of age, was soon added to the number."

There was nothing sensational in that conversion. The man was fifty years old. He lived to be eighty-five, and when he was dying, he said:

"I know whom I have believed. I *know* whom I have believed, and that He is able to keep that which I have committed to Him against that day." Noah Webster found Jesus Christ in his Bible. That made an end of his darkness and doubt. That gave him serenity and confidence. That is the vision we need, and when we have it, the peace of God will keep our minds and hearts.

CHAPTER V.

CRITICISM AND COMMON SENSE.

> "Prove all things; hold fast that which is good."
> —1 THESS. v.: 21.

It is not easy to handle the problems of modern criticism in popular discourse. There are not a few critics who deprecate the introduction of such things into the columns of the secular and religious press, and into the pulpit. Their minute and thorough discussion demands an equipment and training which are wholly foreign to our congregations, and of which even the large majority of our pastors are destitute. The rank and file of the Christian ministry shrink from the debate, simply because of their conscious lack of equipment. I respect the hesitation, but I have no patience with the lack of equipment which necessitates it. For the lack is due to the criminal neglect of the study of the Old Testament in the original Hebrew, and there is no good reason why men who have received the advantages of the full course of study in our theological seminaries, should not be as much at home in the Hebrew, as they are in the Greek The Greek is vastly more difficult than the Hebrew. Technical scholarship, in neither Greek nor Hebrew, is necessary to equip a man for independent judgment upon critical questions. And the present state of things demands nothing more emphatically than that pastors take down their dust-covered Hebrew Bibles, and gird themselves for familiarity with the tongue, whose alphabet and declensions and conjugations many of them have forgotten. They would lose nothing and gain much, if they would sacrifice for five years the reading of newspapers and magazines, until Hebrew ceased to be a mystery.

THE IRREPRESSIBLE CONFLICT.

For the universities and the theological seminaries have not been able to execute the decree of silence. Few men care what the critics may say about the Iliad and Homer, or the integrity of Cicero's orations. Millions care for what they say about Moses and the prophets, and the books which are attributed to them. The pulpits and the press are interested in what is whispered in the university quadrangles. The debate has assumed a popular form, and it is utterly useless to put on sackcloth and ashes. The only thing to do is to meet the new prophets upon their own ground, and to make it clear that they are at sea about their facts, and that their logic is utterly vicious. The defenders of the literary integrity of the Old Testament have not thrust the matter upon the attention of the public. They have not been eager for the fray, because they believe that other and better work can be done, and needs to be done. But when Sumter was fired upon, the nation responded to the call of Father Abraham; and when once the musket was shouldered, we did not stop until the confederacy had collapsed. And when the historical credibility of the Old Testament is assailed, under the plea of giving us a better Bible, we do not propose to turn the other cheek, but to strip for the fight, and answer thrust for thrust, saber stroke for saber stroke. And I wish to say again, with the utmost earnestness and emphasis, that in my strictures, which I mean to make as sharp and severe as language permits, I shall wholly ignore the personal aspects of the controversy, shall avoid all side issues, and confine myself strictly to the fundamental doctrines which the acknowledged leaders of the new school have propounded, in their treatment of the documents of the Old Testament. I am cutting deeper down than any man's qualified utterances and conditional expositions; I am trying to lay bare the foundation-stones upon which the critical structure rests. I am laying the ax at the root of this poisonous tree, leaving the branches to wither of themselves.

It may be well to state what things are not under debate. There is a definite challenge; and no amount of dust should be allowed to veil it. There are several things which must be eliminated from the present discussion.

THINGS THAT MUST BE ELIMINATED FROM BIBLICAL DISCUSSION.

1. One is the nature, the method, and the design of inspiration. That is a theological, not a criti-

cal, problem; and I, for one, refuse at this juncture to so much as touch it.

2. A second concerns the interpretation of any given book in either the Old Testament or the New. I do not care what any man regards as the meaning of Job or Jonah, of Ecclesiastes or the Song of Solomon. The more fundamental question is, whether any of the Old Testament books are worth reading at all. For if they are mainly fictitious, if they are in the main literary inventions and forgeries, it makes no difference what they mean.

3. A third question of subordinate importance is that of the authorship and date of the Old Testament books. Many of them are confessedly anonymous. How many psalms David wrote is a question of little consequence. Whether Ruth is early or late is not a matter of vital importance.

4. A fourth matter of secondary importance is the problem of literary structure; whether the documents are composite or not; whether certain passages are prose or poetry; whether certain books are narrative or drama or parable. Whether the Song of Solomon is an allegorical prophecy or

a love song; whether Job is a narrative or a drama; whether Jonah is history or parable; whether the first three chapters of Genesis are poetic and pictorial in form, or are to be read as literal prose; these, and a hundred questions like them, are matters of comparative indifference.

5. The one and only question is simply this, whether the Pentateuch and the other Old Testament books give us a true account of the times with which they deal, or whether they are a tissue of legendary tales, of literary inventions, of dishonest manipulation of facts, of deliberate and wicked forgeries. I am using plain English; but that is what the criticism of Graf, Kuenen, and Wellhausen amounts to.

HEINRICH EWALD.

Ewald's name is so frequently mentioned in current discussions, that it may be well to outline the critical position of the famous German. He was revolutionary enough in his day, but he has become a back number with the modern school; though it is a good thing for that school that Ewald is dead. He was an irascible fellow, and had a short, sharp, and decisive way of crushing his opponents. He was a man of great learning and penetration; and his great history of Israel is one of the most stimulating and stirring books which any one can read, if he has the patience to go through its eight good-sized volumes. There is one feature of his scholarship, which is somewhat characteristic of the entire school of revolutionary criticism, and that is the frequent offensive assumption of omniscience, and the summary language in which opponents are dealt with. Ewald refers to Ilgen as having failed in his studies of the subject, speaks of the labors of Hupfeld and Knobel as "unsatisfactory and perverse," and declares that the opinions of Hengstenberg, Delitzsch, Keil and Kurtz, "stand below and outside of all science." "Stupidity" is a favorite word with Ewald to designate those who venture to challenge his dicta. In the critical portions of his work, judgments are entered for which no proof whatever is given, enforced simply by his personal authority, of which he permits neither denial nor doubt. Thus, he declares emphatically that writing was unknown before

Moses, and upon that assumption he resolves the entire patriarchal history into a series of myths or legends.

EWALD'S ASSUMPTION DISCREDITED BY RECENT DISCOVERIES.

I need only add that Ewald's assumption has been thoroughly and forever discredited, by the recent discoveries in Egypt and Assyria, and with these discoveries the entire fabric of the legendary character of the narratives in Genesis collapses. Among other surprising corroborations, is the demonstration that the fourteenth chapter of Genesis is rigidly historical, the record of an actual military campaign in which Abraham was the conspicuous figure, while the mysterious figure of Melchizedec is proved to be that of a living prince. The evidence for the first comes from the plains of Assyria; the evidence for the second comes from the valley of the Nile. The critics never did know what to do with that chapter. It has defied all analysis and dissection. It cannot be credited to E, or to J, or to P, or to the Redactor. Even Ewald conceded that it must be pre-Mosaic. But he treats it as legendary. The critics have proved, over and over again, to their own satisfaction, that it is purely fabulous. This was maintained by Nöldeke as late as 1869, little more than twenty-five years ago. To-day as Professor Brown says, "wise exegetes are not doing this. There is too much light out of the east. The sun has risen too high." Bricks have been dug up out of the mounds of Assyria, which antedate the birth of Abraham. And among them are some which give an account of early Babylonian invasions, with mention of Arioch, Ellasar, and Chederlaomer by name.

It is only ten years since the Tell-Amarna tablets were discovered, between Thebes and Memphis, by an Egyptian peasant woman. These tablets contain official letters of great importance, and they belong to the period immediately after the Exodus, during which Joshua was active in the conquest of Southern Palestine. These tablets mention the Hebrews as invaders, and they speak definitely of Jerusalem and of its king, Ebed-Tob, a royal priest, whose name Major Conder translates as Adonizedek, the equivalent of Melchizedec, "king of justice." The way in which

Ebed-'Tob speaks of his right to the throne of Uru-'Salim is highly interesting and suggestive: "Behold, neither my father nor my mother have exalted me in this place; the arm of the Mighty King has caused me to enter the house of my father." So that in Joshua's time Jerusalem was already well known, and its king was a royal priest.

Thus from the sands of the Nile, and from the mounds of Assyria, rise the long buried bricks which prove the fourteenth chapter of Genesis, confidently relegated by the critics to the realm of legend, to be simple, straightforward history. Down goes the whole legendary fabric at a touch, and it is critically certain that Abraham is no myth.

The critical retreat has been steady and sure. First, the pre-Solomonic history was discredited, and even Moses reduced to a shadow; then a halt was made at Moses, and the entire patriarchal record treated as unhistorical; and now the bricks have compelled a further retreat to Abraham. It is pertinent at this point to quote the words of the eminent orientalist, Professor Hommel of Munich:

"The genuineness and authenticity of an account like that in Genesis xiv. involves a sweeping and destructive criticism of the now fashionable view as to the trustworthiness of the Old Testament traditions, and, therefore, this chapter will ever be a stumbling block to those critics who will not allow a single line to be Mosaic, not even the Decalogue and the so-called Book of the Covenant, and accordingly these men for a long time to come will bend their utmost strength, though with little success, to remove this stone of offense from their path." Thus history plants itself squarely and solidly in the fourteenth chapter of Genesis, and if in this chapter the author of Genesis has not drawn upon his imagination, but has simply discharged the duty of a historian, he may fairly be believed to have been equally honest and conscientious in the thirteen preceding chapters. This conclusion is confirmed by the singular fact, that the Assyrian inscriptions have made it certain that Nimrod is not a myth, but a historical figure.

EWALD'S PARTITION.

But to return to Ewald's critical partition of

the Pentateuch, or of the Hexateuch, as it is now called. He discovered eight sources and names them as follows:

1. The Book of the Wars of Jahveh, containing brief sketches of military exploits under Moses and Joshua, composed soon after Joshua's death.

2. The Biography of Moses, giving the main facts in the life of the great lawgiver, and composed within the first century after the death of Joshua.

3. The Book of Covenants, located in the period of Samson.

4. The Book of Origins, which Ewald makes to include the Levitical legislation, which he refers to Solomon's time, and regards as embodying in fixed form the ritual of the Tabernacle. This book excites his profound admiration, and he concludes its study in these words:

"Lofty spirit! thou whose work has for centuries not unnaturally had the fortune of being taken for that of thy great hero, Moses, himself, I know not thy name and divine only from thy vestiges when thou didst live and what thou didst achieve, but if these thy traces incontrovertibly forbid me to identify thee with him who was greater than thou, and whom thou thyself only desiredst to magnify according to his deserts, then see that there is no guile in me, nor any pleasure in knowing thee not absolutely as thou wast." Men may, if they choose, call that eloquence, as some have done; I call it unmitigated sentimental bosh and bombast.

5. The third narrator, belonging to Northern Palestine, and appearing soon after the Book of Origins.

6. The fourth narrator, belonging to Southern Palestine, and living in the ninth century, B. C.

7. The fifth narrator, belonging to Southern Palestine, and living in the eighth century, B. C.

8. The Deuteronomist, located in the middle part of the seventh century, B. C., about thirty years before Hilkiah's discovery of the Book of the Law, which Ewald declares was written by the Deuteronomist in Egypt. Ewald declares that the phrase by which the book is described is indefinite, and means no more than "a law book," but every tyro in Hebrew knows better, and the

phrase can only mean, as Strack insists, *a* writing or written copy of *the* Law; that is, the only, authoritative, well-known Law.

These are certainly amazing discoveries. Ewald may be right, but we have nothing for it but his word. His hypothesis is known as the crystalization theory. His idea is, that the literary basis of the Hexateuch is the first document mentioned, which the second writer embodied, recast and enlarged, the third following in the steps of his predecessors, until the Deuteronomist completed the task. There are different layers in the literary structure, of which the Book of Origins is the most remarkable, but there is original literary unity in the final result. At each successive stage the preceding narratives were vitally incorporated, so that we have not a series of scissored fragments, or of supplementary additions. Ewald insists that criticism must recognize and explain the unity of the Pentateuch. And upon the central problem of modern criticism, the date of the middle books of the Pentateuch, the document now called P., or the Priest-code, which is declared to belong to the period of the second temple, 450 B. C., the great authority of Ewald comes down like a sledge hammer. His argument is massive and convincing, that it cannot be later than David or Solomon, that it is the Law Book of the first temple, and that it only codified and made fixed the ritual of the tabernacle, which the temple of Solomon displaced.

GENERAL FEATURES OF THE NEW CRITICISM.

Now, while I cannot enter into the details of the current discussion, I can outline its main general features; and the reader can judge for himself to how much of serious confidence the new criticism is entitled. There are five affirmations upon which the critics proceed, and which they embody in their creed.

1. They insist upon eliminating all miraculous elements from the Pentateuch. Very well; then all such elements must be cut out of the New Testament. I do not insist that a man shall and must believe in the literalness of the Jonah story; I do insist that if he rejects it simply because it is a miracle, he has no good reason for believing

that Jesus Christ was born of a virgin, or that He rose from the dead.

2. They insist upon the mythical character of the patriarchal narratives. As I have already said, the curious confirmation of the historical character of the fourteenth chapter of Genesis, leaves that theory no peg to hang on. Abraham is as real a figure as Moses.

3. They insist upon the legendary character of the Mosaic and the post-Mosaic history, which we are assured was very different from what the books represent it; and that even Hosea did not know what he was talking about. Upon that I make no comment. It needs none.

4. They insist that Deuteronomy was not written until 900 years after Moses, and that the entire account of the addresses which he is represented as giving, is fictitious. Ewald protests against the suggestion that Hilkiah forged the document; but the present critics are not so sensitive. Upon that I make no comment. It needs none.

5. They insist that the legislation which makes up the larger part of the middle books of the

Pentateuch, and which is habitually introduced by the phrase: "The Lord said unto Moses," so affirming plainly and frequently its Mosaic origin, was inoperative and unknown for a thousand years after the great lawgiver's death, and was the product of Ezekiel and Ezra, about 450 B. C. The document, embodying this legislation, was called the "Book of Origins," by Ewald, but has been more generally spoken of as the work of the Elohist, and now passes under the title of the Priest-code, and is designated by the letter P.

It had been the unanimous judgment of scholars, that this document was the oldest of the two main documents which make up the Pentateuch. It was claimed that its classical style proved its high antiquity, and that its narrative portions were invested with the highest credibility. The first chapter of Genesis belongs to this document. In 1866 Graf, who had been a pupil of Reuss, startled the learned world by reversing this unanimous verdict, separating the legal from the historical portions of the Elohist document, and maintaining that the laws were not enacted before the Exile. He admitted, however, the antiquity of the narratives. He was soon reminded that the two parts were so closely interwoven, that both must share a common fortune, and, without an instant's hesitation, Graf announced that the history must go down with the laws. The classical style of the document could not save it, a fact which it is well to remember when the critics use that argument upon other occasions. The Dutch critic, Kuenen, who had been powerfully influenced by Colenso, promptly gave the new theory his earnest and aggressive support; but it was not until 1878, when Wellhausen gave it his indorsement, that it secured any considerable following, and during all these years it has been vigorously challenged and opposed upon scholarly grounds.

Reuss, George, Vatke, and Popper had anticipated the new critics, the former by more than thirty years. Bleek, Ryssel, Schrader, Klostermann, Baudissen, Kay, Kleinert, Dillmann, Delitzch, Strack, Hoffmann, Orelli, Oehler, Keil, Riehm, Buhl, Hommel, Böhl, Bredenkampf, Marti, Kittel, König, Zahn, Rupprecht, and

Hoedemaker may be mentioned as emphatically condemning the main positions of this school, whose most recent leaders are Kuenen and Wellhausen. Of those I have named, the last four have published their strictures since 1894. English and American scholarship, defending the conservative position, is represented by Davidson, Pusey, Stanley, Duff, Geikie, Watson, Sime, Binnie, Watts, Cave, Ellicott, Leathes, Simon, Orr, Dods, Rainy, Robertson, French, Sayce, Cotterill, McClintock, Strong, Bissell, Vos, Mead, Dwinell, Trumbull, Bartlett, Curtiss, Ladd, Chambers, Green, Osgood, Stebbins, Gardiner, Schodde, Terry, Steinert, Denio, Zenos, Beattie, Morse, Warfield, and Willis J. Beecher. This list of seventy names belongs wholly to the last fifty years, and the greater part to the last twenty-five years.

Besides, it has been made so perfectly plain that many of the Levitical laws are older than the period of Josiah, and that some of them are even pre-Mosaic, that many of the critics have been forced to admit that the Priest-code embodies legislation of the highest antiquity, and is not to be regarded as a document manufactured by the priests of Ezra's time, but as a compilation and recodification of ancient regulations, both written and traditional. This is the contention of Driver and Briggs. This concession is the thin edge of the wedge, which must ultimately split the Wellhausen theory into fragments. The dissection of the Pentateuch is not an easy task; but it is child's play compared with the attempt to break up the Priest-code into successive layers of legislation. The code is compact, so uniform in literary structure that it cannot be divided into old and new. Besides, the separate sections are introduced by the uniform formula: "The Lord said unto Moses," which must be held to be true of all, or true of none, unless we are prepared to grant that the critic can infallibly determine where the statement is true, and where it is false. Moreover, the legislation is imbedded in a narrative which is located in the time of Moses, and which embodies such facts as the Exodus, the giving of the Law at Sinai, the building of the tabernacle, the provision of manna, the consecration of Aaron to the priesthood, the death of

Nadab and Abihu for violating the law prescribing the offering of incense, the numbering of the people, the dedication of the sanctuary, the murmurings of the Israelites, the leprosy of Miriam, the mission of the spies, the stoning of the Sabbath breaker, the judgment upon Korah, Dathan, and Abiram, the blossoming of Aaron's rod, the miraculous supply of water, the death of Aaron, the story of Balak and Balaam, the zeal of Phinehas, and the appointment of Joshua as the successor of Moses. These narratives and the laws are woven together. If the narratives are true, the laws are old, and of Mosaic origin, enacted during the forty years which cover the wilderness life. If the laws belong in large part to the time of Ezra, a thousand years later, the narratives must be fictitious, deliberately invented to give a plausible coloring of Mosaic authority to the laws. Reuss is brutally frank when he tells us that the history is a "base fiction, the dream of an impoverished race;" and Kuenen and Wellhausen declare the narratives to be thoroughly unhistorical and unreliable.

EVIDENCE ADDUCED IN BEHALF OF ADVERSE PENTATEUCHAL CRITICISM.

The only tangible evidence offered in support of a claim which carries such conclusions with it, which makes the Pentateuchal history a conscious and deliberate fraud and forgery, is drawn from the historical books, which show that for many centuries after Moses the laws of the Priest-code were not enforced. This general non-observance is construed as proving that such a law could not have been known, and that it could not have been in existence. And yet, we read of the sanctuary and ark at Shiloh, and of the high priest there, and of sacrifices offered there. We read also of the national grief and despair when the ark was captured, and of the national joy when another resting place was secured for it. We have a long account of the building of the temple by Solomon, and of the impressive magnificence of its dedication. We do not read of many arks, nor of many tabernacles, nor of many temples. The worship appears as centralized in the days of Samuel, David, and Solomon; and throughout the succeeding record, sacrifice on the high places is spoken of in terms of condemnation. Samuel's sacrifice at Mizpeh and Bethlehem, and Elijah's sacrifice on Mount Carmel, have been adduced to prove the contrary. But the circumstances were extraordinary, and no permanent altars were erected. In Samuel's case the ark had been captured, and that made an end of Shiloh as a sanctuary. Sacrifice could be offered only where God's prophet happened to be; for, Shiloh having been deserted by God, He could be present only in the person of His prophet. And the same fact explains the action of Elijah on Mount Carmel, for in the kingdom of Northern Palestine there never had been, and could not be, an authorized sanctuary. These instances do not contradict the law in Deuteronomy and Leviticus, which limits sacrifice to the place which the Lord should choose. No definite place was mentioned, and when none existed, as in the case of Samuel and of Elijah, the prophet was the only man with whom the choice of place rested. The old maxim, "*exceptio probat regulam*" applies here. The exceptional and extraordinary instances prove that the general law was well known, and was respected. Under the monarchy, and after the middle of Solomon's reign, sacrifices on the high places gained entrance and were stubbornly persisted in; but the ark and the temple remained as the central rallying place, a standing protest against the multiplication of altars.

THE REAL HISTORY.

Taking the history as a whole, and treating it in the way of general credibility, refusing to regard it as self-contradictory, we find that after the removal of the ark to Jerusalem, and after the building of the Temple by Solomon, sacrifice upon the high places is always recorded as unauthorized and condemnable. There was a central sanctuary, and a single authorized altar. In the early periods of Samuel's life, the record speaks of the sanctuary and the ark at Shiloh, as the sacrificial rallying point of the nation, and there is no intimation that there was any other. Then came the capture of the ark by the Philistines, as the judgment of God upon the sons of Eli, who had defiled and disgraced the priesthood. That made an end of Shiloh. Seven months the ark remained in captivity, and then it was returned to Kirjath-Jearim; but while the priests and the diviners were consulted, and took part in the restoration, Samuel does not appear as having any share in the arrangements. The return of the ark did not remove the Divine displeasure; and the prophet of God was silent, which was an ominous sign. He shunned the ark, and this neglect continued, as we are informed, for twenty years. When at last David ventured to remove it from Kirjath-Jearim, after Samuel's death, he was interrupted by the death of Uzzah; and, interpreting this as evidence of God's displeasure, the king feared to carry out his plans, and left the ark in the house of Obed-Edom. There the ark remained for three months, and brought with it a blessing to the home of Obed-Edom. When David learned this fact, he interpreted it as a sign that his original purpose was approved of God, and he promptly brought the ark into Jerusalem with great and eager joy. The lesson is plain and unmistakable; for more than twenty years there was no divinely recognized sanctuary; and in view of its former existence at Shiloh, and its later establishment at Jerusalem, we must conclude that there must have been good reasons for the twenty years during which there was no fixed place of sacrifice. Samuel went neither to Shiloh, where the ark had been, nor to Kirjath-Jearim, where the ark was; but sacrificed at Mizpeh or Gilgal or Bethlehem, as his judgment dictated. He simply fell back upon the earlier patriarchal practise, until the Divine displeasure should have passed away. This is a perfectly natural explanation, and does not array one part of the history against the other; for when that is done, it must be impossible to determine what were the real facts.

In the case of Elijah the exceptional condition of things is even more evident. Northern Israel never had an authorized sanctuary, nor a legitimate priesthood. When Jeroboam seceded, he built altars at Dan and at Bethel; but the record which makes mention of the fact, also discloses the fact that Jerusalem was regarded as the only lawful place of sacrifice, and further declares that Jeroboam was guilty of idolatry, and was publicly rebuked by a prophet of God. In such a condition of religious anarchy, a prophet like Elijah could only take counsel with himself, as to when and where it was proper for him to sacrifice. The cases are plainly exceptional, and they have their place in a narrative which discloses a central and exclusive sanctuary at Shiloh, and at Jerusalem; so that the record itself contradicts the interpretation of the critics. To claim that such exceptional cases illustrate the ancient, ordinary, and universal practise; and upon the ground of such an assumption, to cast wholesale discredit upon the historical setting of Deuteronomy, and of the middle books of the Pentateuch, is an outrage upon all canons of sober criticism, and is entitled to no courtesy of treatment. No reason can be given why one part of the record should be regarded as infallibly correct, while the other is dismissed as having been inserted by the hand of a later writer, who was so stupid as not to see that his own additions squarely contradicted the story which he copied. There is just as good ground for affirming that Samuel never sacrificed at Mizpeh, Gilgal, and Bethlehem, and that Elijah never built an altar upon Mount Carmel, as that a central and exclusively authorized sanctuary did not exist in the time of the Judges and the Kings. The only consistent thing to do, is either to take the record as it stands and harmonize its statements, or to stamp the whole of it as unreliable and unworthy of credence. The assumption of the critics that the sacrificial worship was not authoritatively centralized and limited until the eighteenth year of Josiah, about 622 B. C., cannot be made out without discrediting in large part the historical books to which they appeal.

And this they do not hesitate to do. The narratives in the Pentateuch are declared to be fictitious, and the literary inventions of a late day. The books of Joshua and Judges fare no better. Samuel and Kings have been tampered with. Chronicles is purely fictitious history. It represents only what was believed and taught by the priests in the fourth century B. C. The prophets, too, were the victims of the same hallucination. They did not know the real history. They were mistaken when they represented Israel as guilty of disobedience and apostasy. Their burning zeal outran their knowledge. What now remains of the Old Testament literature as a record of historical facts? Nothing, absolutely nothing. The critics have cut the ground from under their own feet. They use Samuel and Kings to discredit the Pentateuch, but they cannot even do that without casting discredit upon Samuel and Kings. For as the record stands, it flatly contradicts, at many points of the narrative, and in the most incidental way, the theory that Deuteronomy was unknown during the period of the Judges and the major part of the monarchy, and that sacrifice on the high places was not regarded as unauthorized. The discrepancy is removed by maintaining, and attempting to prove, that Joshua, Judges, Samuel, and Kings, exist only in the Deuteronomic redaction, and by the easy process of crediting all obnoxious passages to the Deuteronomic editor, the critics claim that the narrative proves that the Deuteronomic law was unknown. They rely upon the prophets to drag Moses from his seat, and to do that they must charge the prophets with ignorance. They appeal to the historians to discredit the priests, and to do that they must decimate the work of the historians. Is that science? Are such statements and charges to be accepted as a matter of course, and to be listened to in patience? They are entitled only to lightning condemnation.

HISTORY OF THE OLD TESTAMENT AS RECONSTRUCTED BY THE CRITICS.

Let me sketch, as far as I may be able, the real history of the Old Testament religion, as the critics construct it after having decimated the documents, and involved them in general discredit. I leave my reader to judge how much confidence can be reasonably given to critical methods, which conduct to such a result. Genesis, from cover to cover, is treated as a mass of popular sagas and legends, ranking with the pagan mythologies and heroic tales. The patriarchal history is dissolved into literary fiction. Wellhausen concedes that a small body of men and women, under the leadership of Moses, marched out of Egypt, through the wilderness; and across the Jordan, under Joshua, into Canaan. Stade will not admit even this; Jülicher treats the whole story of the plagues with sarcastic contempt. And all the critics are agreed that whatever the real facts may have been, they have become almost unrecognizable, because of the miraculous coloring, which, of course, is wholly fictitious. Covenant with Abraham there was none, the vocation of Moses is the fanciful sketch of a late age, the passage of the Red Sea is incredible, the manna never fell, the forty years of desert life are a pure invention. Moses died, of course, but he never delivered, in the plains of Moab, the discourses which are attributed to him. The books of Joshua and of Judges are as unreliable as the Pentateuch. We do not reach firm, historical ground, until we come to the time of Solomon, though even here we must sift our authorities. The history as recorded in Kings has been tampered with, and Chronicles is regarded as practically worthless. Monotheism was not the original creed of the nation. The word Elohim points to a polytheistic period. Jehovah was simply the tribal and national God. The temple and the high places represented two parties in the national religion, neither of which could rightly claim priority or exclusive authority. With Hosea and Amos the monotheistic party seized the theological leadership, and after two hundred years secured practical ascendancy. This led to the centralization of the national worship, of which Deuteronomy was the literary measure and result. Then came the destruction of the temple, and during the captivity the priests elaborated a code, which Ezra brought with him to Jerusalem and completed about the middle of the fifth century, B. C. Thus, the theology of the Old Testament was the creation of the prophets of the ninth and eighth centuries, B. C., and the priests of Ezra's time organized the ritual of the sanctuary. On its face, the Book of Job is located in a primitive state of society, but the theology of Job is high, and its monotheism is pronounced; therefore, in spite of style and coloring, it is dragged down to a late date. Proverbs and Ecclesiastes share the same fate. The decided monotheism of the Psalter leads the critics to push not only the collection of the psalms, but their composition, to the period of the second temple. Ewald leaves thirteen psalms to

David, but refuses to credit him with the Twenty-third and the Fifty-first psalms; and Ewald is more than usually generous; the general disposition is to deny all Davidic authorship. All that is high in theological tone, or reflects an orderly and ordered form of worship, is assumed to be of late origin—the product of a period which, when judged by the literary remnants left us in the Apocryphal books, was destitute of genius, narrow in its outlook, and stupid in childish superstition. This is called a reconstruction of Israel's history; it is simply its demolition; and the result is a travesty of criticism.

ORDER OF THE CODES.

This construction of Israel's history depends entirely upon the assumption, that the order of the Pentateuchal Codes begins with the Book of the Covenant, which includes the laws recorded in Exodus xx.: 18—xxiii.: 33. From that point we must jump over Leviticus and Numbers, and find the second Code of laws in Deuteronomy. Then we must leap back again to Exodus xxiv., at which point the final and most elaborate **Code** begins. The Book of the Covenant is supposed to be Mosaic, the basis of the Sinai and wilderness organization. The Deuteronomic Code is located in the time of Josiah, about 622 B. C. The Priest-code is nearly two hundred years later, the combined work of Ezekiel and Ezra, about 440 B. C. This arrangement violently dislocates the literary material as it lies before us, and makes the narrative portions of the Priest-code utterly misleading and unreliable. At the same time the Decalogue is left hanging in air. Its most natural place would be in the Book of the Covenant. But to locate it there would overturn the entire critical structure. For Genesis i. : 1—ii. : 4, is declared to be from the hand of P., who wrote in Ezra's time. But in the fourth commandment there is an unmistakable reference to the creation story in Genesis; and to admit that the Decalogue belongs to the first Code of laws, would be to grant that the contents of the creation story were already known and current in their present form; which, of course, would make havoc of the entire critical contention. It is an awkward thing for the critics, that there should be any Decalogue at all, especially to find it inserted where it is. The order of Codes which the narrative indicates, is the Decalogue first, as the foundation of the entire legislation ; next the Book of the Covenant, with its few and simple regulations ; next the Priest-code entering more fully into the details of worship and life ; and, finally, the Deuteronomic summary and modifications, made necessary by the near settlement in Canaan. This is the natural order, corresponding exactly to the historical setting, doing no violence to the material, and giving to the Decalogue its commanding place. In wrenching the Decalogue from the Law Book, the critics simply decapitate the legislation, and leave it a mutilated and ghastly trunk ; and with the legislation goes the history !

SOURCES OF INFORMATION WORTHY OF CREDENCE.

The first canon of historical criticism is, that the sources which are consulted and examined shall be treated as entitled to belief. If divergencies are found, the elements of common agreement must be searched for, and made the foundation of the historical narrative. Nor must the discrepancies be interpreted as contradictions, but as the partial reports of equally honest witnesses or writers. The charge of falsehood is the very last one which should be made or entertained. This is the method of every great historian. And if, as is often the case, he finds it impossible to harmonize divergent accounts, he simply acknowledges the fact, without even hinting the charge of dishonesty. Much less would he assume that all the available documents had been tampered with, in the interest of more or less deliberate deception. Such a procedure would be laughed out of court in secular history. But the radical critics make such a procedure in dealing with the Old Testament books fundamental. The historical books are arrayed against the Pentateuch, and especially against the Priest-code. Whatever in the historical books does not square with the theory, is declared to be the work of a later writer, who invented the facts to support his own view. Some one, steeped in the philosophy and theology of Deuteronomy, which is assumed to have been produced in the seventh century, B.C., is declared to have thrust his views into the entire literature, from Moses to Chronicles, and the prophets themselves are regarded as victims of the same hallucination. The result is expressed in the phrase "idealized history," which is applied with equal facility to Jonah, Judges, Exodus, Samuel, and Kings. And in plain speech, idealized history is idealized nonsense. It simply means fiction and fable. The man who invents his facts, or distorts them, is not a man who can be trusted in telling us what the invented facts mean. It is serious enough to find the critics denying all miracle and prophecy as absolutely incredible, and reducing the supernatural to a religious estimate of the purely natural, but it is tenfold more serious to reduce the Old Testament to a warring camp, in which the writers slaughter each other, and fall upon their own swords. But the critics have no option in the matter. The documents must be discredited to make their theory good. For if the facts were as they are stated, the revolutionary criticism is thoroughly discredited; and if the facts were not as they are stated, the attempted reconstruction is a waste of ingenuity, and we might as well consign the Old Testament to our garrets or cellars, as unworthy of any serious historical study.

It is not a question of inerrancy here; it is not a question of discrepancies in detailed description; it is not a question of geography, of numbers, and of chronologies; the claim is that the history is fabricated and false, from cover to cover; and that the real facts are the very reverse from the account given in the Old Testament. Mistakes the most accurate and painstaking historian may make, and does make. And it is not necessary to assume that inspiration secured photographic inerrancy. But it requires no argument to prove, that a historian who deliberately invents his facts, and who gives a thoroughly false picture of the times which he describes, cannot be honest, much less inspired. He may be honest and trustworthy, without being inspired; but he cannot be inspired, and yet be dishonest and a false witness. An inspiration defended at the cost of honesty, is an insult to man, and it is blasphemy against God. I do not know that the denial of inspiration would seriously disturb me, so long as the truth of the Biblical record is conceded and assured. If the Bible is true — that is all for which I care. But if the Biblical history is fabricated and false, I resent all cheap and sentimental talk about inspiration and revelation. Lies do not come from God; they are Satanic in origin and contents; and if it can be made clear to me that the Pentateuchal narrative is, as Reuss says, "a base fiction," then I shall be consistent enough to declare that the Old Testament is the devil's book, and not God's.

Nor, upon such a theory, have I any use for the New Testament, which grows from the same stock. For if there be falsehood in the tap root, the poison must be in every twig, leaf, bud, and blossom. This cannot be a tree of life, but a tree of death. The conclusion is startling, but I do not see how it can be evaded; and when I see how this revolutionary criticism has gone to pieces when it has laid hands upon the New Testament, I feel assured that its lances will break when they touch the older Scriptures. For myself, I insist that when the new school declares Deuteronomy to be the literary invention of the seventh century B. C., and the Levitical legislation to be the literary invention of the fifth century B. C., they have not a shred of evidence upon which to rest, and their treatment of the documents and of their authors is such as to arouse the indignant remonstrance of all who are not prepared to charge the Old Testament writers with wholesale falsehood. A charge so outrageous thrusts the sword into its own vitals.

CRITICISM AND COMMON SENSE.

And there is just one thing more I want to say, and to say it as emphatically as I can. Nearly eighty years ago, in 1819, Archbishop Whateley, then a fellow in Oriel College and thirty-two years of age, made the skeptical school of his time the target of his wit by arguing, with apparent seriousness, that nothing was positively known concerning the life of Napoleon Bonaparte, and that it was somewhat doubtful whether such a man ever lived. Of course, everybody laughed, except the critics. A few years ago one of our American scholars, then residing in Germany, dissected the Epistle to the

Romans, as the critics do the Pentateuch, and made out a very good case that several documents could clearly be traced in its structure. Of course, many laughed; the critics sneered, but they winced as they sneered. Professor Green has shown that it is as easy to make out the dual structure of the parable of the prodigal son, as to dissect the story of Joseph into two interwoven narratives. There is not an oration, or essay, or poem, which could not be shown to be composite in its structure. The *Interior* of Chicago reports that "the editor of a Baptist paper in Waco, Tex., finds it easier to believe in two Harpers than in two Isaiahs. The style of Isaiah xl. may be quite different from the style of Isaiah xxxix., but the assertions of President Harper in one part of his writings are contradicted by assertions in what follows. In one part of his essay he says that the early chapters of Genesis constitute 'the beginning of history,' and in another that these chapters 'contain neither history nor geography.' In one place he says that the writer of these chapters 'takes the stories common to all ancient nations,' and in another place, that the book is a 'compilation from written sources, not one of which goes back to the days of Solomon.'" And the Waco Baptist editor concludes "Our critics do not agree with each other, but that is no reason why one of them should get into a shindy with himself."

Nor has any great history ever been written, where a microscopic criticism could not discover inaccuracies, and discrepancies, and want of full information, and where these could not be used to discredit the entire story, and convict the writer either of ignorance or of wilful deception. Such criticism outrages common sense, and common sense is needed in the critical study of the Bible. It is a wise maxim of the law, that a man shall be deemed innocent until he has been proved guilty. It is a wise maxim of literary criticism, that the historian must be assumed to be honest and worthy of confidence. And all the more must this hold true, when we find that his writings have had wide circulation from very early times, and that during all these centuries they have been regarded with profoundest veneration by a most remarkable people, whose ancestry is lost in the depths of antiquity. If we make the Old Testament false, what shall we do with the Jews, whose fortunes are traced in these Scriptures, and whose law they still reverence and obey? To suppose that their history for more than 2,300 years, since Ezra's time, has been based upon faith in fabricated documents, makes a somewhat large demand upon credulity. It argues a criminal audacity in the priesthood of Ezra's day, and a dense stupidity on the part of the people, which are simply incredible. A sober judgment will conclude that the nation must be believed in the account which it has given us of its history, and that its documentary literature is entitled to respectful and honorable treatment.

And this judgment is made all the more imperative, when we consider that this people and its literature have been the preachers of the world's righteousness and redemption. They have given us the Law and the Gospel. They have given us Moses and Christ. Such men are not the products of a race nourished upon falsehood. I do not say that as a bar to criticism. I want such criticism to be thorough and searching, but I insist that an irreverent and slanderous criticism should be resented by every man who finds any good in Christianity, and who does not believe that men have been dupes and fools for two and a half milleniums. "*Prove all things*," yes, but do not forget what follows: "*Hold fast that which is good.*" There is none too much of it in the world!

CHAPTER VI.

THE HISTORIC FAITH.

> "Let us therefore, as many as be perfect, be thus minded; and if in anything ye be otherwise minded, God shall reveal even this unto you. Nevertheless, whereto we have already attained, let us walk by the same rule, let us mind the same thing."
> —PHILIPPIANS iii. : 15-16.

WE are all more or less disposed, at times at least, to yield to the temptation against which the Christians in Philippi were earnestly and affectionately warned — magnifying the things in which we differ, and ignoring or underestimating the things in which we agree. To many the history of Christianity seems hardly more than a sad succession of bitter controversies, rending the seamless garment of the unity for which our Lord prayed ; and the prophets of what is called organic unity do not seem to meet with much encouragement. Not only is Christendom divided ; but Christendom seems determined to remain divided. Rome extends the olive branch of peace to the Greek Church; but the Greek Church answers with lofty disdain. Canterbury makes advances to the Greek Church, and to the Roman Church; both answer in the negative with almost brutal frankness. The House of Bishops presents a plan of union for all the forces of Protestantism; and when we come to examine it, it simply means, in plain English, that if we will consent to receive episcopal confirmation and ordination, we may all come into the Episcopal Church. Meanwhile, the Baptist quietly tells us that he cannot consent to enter into such a partnership, unless we are all immersed, and surrender infant baptism. The lion is perfectly willing that the lamb and he shall lie down together, if only the poor lamb will consent to lie inside the lion. All this provokes the scorn of some, and it pains many more. It seems as if Christians did not care to be one.

THE TRUE UNITY.

But sometimes we search among the stars for that which lies at our feet. In the Republic of Plato, Socrates starts the question "What is Justice?" and a long debate ensues, in which the participants become confused; when suddenly the great teacher cries: "So here it lies at our feet — justice is simply every man doing his own work." I am afraid that many of us are making the same mistake. The angel of unity is our pillar of cloud and fire, and always has been; and we know it not. We ache and pray for that which has already come. Can it be that our Lord's prayer has remained unanswered all these centuries? For myself, at least, the years have taught me, that we need to say "*we are one*," as well as to pray that we may be one. I have learned that the unities of the Christian faith are more mighty and majestic than the differences. I have grasped the hand of many a Roman Catholic layman and priest, when at the clasp of palms and mutual greetings the yawning chasm vanished; and if I had to choose between Pope Leo XIII., and Confucius, I should not hesitate a moment.

UNIFORMITY IMPOSSIBLE.

But look at the warring sects, you say. It is, I confess, a pitiable sight. But point me to the time, if you can, when sharp differences did not exist. You cannot. They were as pronounced and fierce in the apostolic churches as they are to-day. A decade had scarcely passed when a council had to be called at Jerusalem, and the famous decrees settled nothing. They were a rope of sand. The fire blazed out anew at Antioch, and it became a conflagration in the churches of Galatia, rousing Paul into unwonted wrath — when he hurled anathemas upon his opponents. The word "*nevertheless,*" in Paul's exhortation to the Philippians, is an open window, through which we discover that controversy was not unknown in Philippi even. It rent the church at Corinth into parties. In every epistle the same fact obtrudes. There have always been sharp doctrinal and ritual differences, and there always will be. But these very differences, when traced to their root, will always be found to have been fibered upon a unity of confession, which, like the tides of the sea, has carried all before it.

Honest differences of opinion are not ground for despondency. They are inevitable, where thought is vital. They could not be prevented if we tried ; and we ought not to try, if we were sure of success. Dead men do not quarrel ; but a lively debating society is better than a graveyard. We might as well complain that light is not one, because it breaks into the colors of the rainbow. Light is a wizard, gifted with infinite sleight of hand, as it broods over cloud, and mountain, and sea, performing a thousand fantastic feats ; but in its invisible ground it is always the same. The same pulsations in the air create the sighing of the wind, the roar of the breakers, the crash of the thunder-peal, the cry of agony, the sweet song of nightingale and lark ; and the same pulsations weave the ever fleeting colors with which the universe is radiant. So there come times in the history of a people when some great crisis snaps the ties of party allegiance ; and, as when the ocean is laid bare by a storm, we see the common patriotism which is the bedrock of national unity. We are always dividing, and we divide without loss of unity. It must always be so.

It is the law of the human mind. It is more. It is the law of God. He does not live on the dead level of uniformity. He is one, but He is also infinite. His reason is immutable, but His thoughts are multitudinous, and past finding out. Their apparent antagonisms, crowding to the front in every sphere, confound us. His power and will are one; but His executive acts are infinite. The eternal unity directs the endless manifestations. And the law of His personal being is inserted into the work of His hands. As we mount from lowest to highest, in the scale of being, the differences multiply. One drop of water is like every other drop; all grains of sand are alike; but even these take on endless forms in coast outline and mountain aspect. With life a greater diversity appears. The unity breaks out into an endless variety of form and color. The unity breaks *out*, it does not break *up*. No two leaves are alike, growing from the same stem. No two flowers are alike, growing from the same slender and swaying stock. In the human body the differentiation reaches its highest known form. In the human brain alone there are said to be two thousand million cells. It would take seventy-five years to count them, with three hundred and sixty-five working days of ten hours each. The complexity is bewildering to the keenest eye; the unity is patent to all. We seek for uniformity in Christian thought; when, to secure it, would be to cut ourselves loose from the law of the universe, and from the law of God. It is not the elimination of differences which we are to seek; but the maintenance of unity in the differences,— walking by the same rule, minding — that is intent upon — the same thing. The rule is Christ; the thing is our salvation.

THE HISTORIC FAITH.

There is a common Christian creed. There is an immutable Christian confession. It never has been eclipsed, and it never can be. There is an apostolic unity which has never been broken; and its main features are easily traced. There is but one foundation; none other can be laid; and no church has ever ventured to build upon any other. Let us briefly trace its outlines. Let me enumerate a few of the great common Christian convictions, compared with which our differences are trivial.

MONOTHEISM.

And first, there is the fundamental confession of the One, Living, Only True God. Monotheism has been the creed of our infancy. It is in the air we breathe. But monotheism represents the most radical and far-reaching intellectual revolution which history records. The first verse of Genesis is the simplest and the sublimest sentence ever written by the hand of man; — and Israel's great achievement is that its monotheistic confession has displaced idolatry and polytheism. The conception of God as personal, as self-existent, self-conscious, and self-revealing, is basic and determining in religion. Its sharp accentuation is the universal and permanent need. For while idolatry and polytheism have disappeared, the ghost of pantheism lingers. In much of our poetry and philosophy, God figures only as the ground of being, as impersonal and unconscious force, as blind energy or will, as an Infinite *It*, rather than the eternal *I am*. "*I AM*," that is God,— self-conscious, self-consistent, self-revealing; as personal and individual, as am I. The lines of battle have raged between transcendence and immanence. I care very little for the words. What I want to know is, whether above the world or in it, God is *I am*, personal Being. For if God be self-conscious and self-revealing personal Being,— the path is open between Him and me. He can speak to me, and I can pray to Him. Religion vanishes if man cannot come to God ; and revelation vanishes if God cannot come to man ; both religion and revelation are secure if God be the Eternal *I am*, self-conscious and self-revealing. And in these days, when theosophy makes dupes of some, and monism entangles others, both of them thinly disguised pantheism, the breezy and invigorating Christian affirmation of God as the Living One needs sharp and continuous utterance.

THE LAW OF GOD.

Equally important and valuable is the common Christian confession, that the Personal God is supreme and sovereign. His will is the Law of the universe. To that will all must bow in glad obedience. It is not an arbitrary will. It is not an artificial law. The will and the law are the expression of Infinite Reason. They cannot be other than they are. And hence they are immutable. They cannot be changed by a jot or tittle. We must measure up to their level. The law of God is holy and good. Its requirements are beneficent. We think of Duty as a burden and a badge of service; Duty is the dignity of rational existence, and our badge of honor. It is Duty which makes us divine. It is the conscience of Duty which make the difference between stars and souls; and the glory of a soul is when it moves without weariness and with gladness in the orbit of Duty. The *ought* makes our manhood and womanhood. There never was a great nature without reverence for the law of God. There never was a great nation without reverence for righteousness. Need I refer to the widespread disregard of law, and contempt for it? Statutes are defied and evaded as soon as they are enacted. Men talk as if law could be made and unmade at will, without any reference to the eternal verities embodied in nature and in the soul of man. There is slight reverence for legislatures, for Congress, for judicial decisions; and the contempt is often justifiable. All the greater is the need that the majesty of the moral law should suffer no eclipse. There are some things which cannot be defied. The law of God cannot be trampled upon with impunity. Its violation is a crime of the highest magnitude. It is rebellion, and it is suicide. The way of obedience is the way of life. All crave to be happy, but there can be no blessedness, here or hereafter, unless it grow upon the fiber of holiness.

CHRIST THE ONLY SAVIOR.

A third great confession in which Christendom has always been agreed, is that Jesus Christ came to save sinners. The law condemns us all, so that there is no difference. We are shut up to the undeserved mercy of God. By grace must we be saved. Not merely pardoned, but renewed, and cleansed, and sanctified in body, soul, and spirit. For Christ does not set aside the law of God. He fulfils it in Himself, and dwelling in us by His Spirit He fulfils it in us. Faith in Christ is surrender to Him. Surrender to Him is making His will our own. He always willed what the law of God enacted; and if we surrender our will to His will, we will what the law of God enacts. That frees us from the Law as a taskmaster, and that is the only way out of bondage. We must will what the law enjoins. But that is only the first step. To will what the Law enjoins is one thing; to do what we thus will is a very different thing. For the will in every one of us is weak. But the faith by which we trust in Him, and surrender ourselves to Him, allies us to the perfect obedience which His will secured. There is no magic in the process. It is simply the power of His personal influence, steadily exerted upon our obedient minds and hearts. With open face beholding Him, we are changed into His image. The change is not of our production; *He* changes us; but we must fix our eyes upon Him. We must abide in Him, as the branch abides in the vine. This is no theory of the atonement. In the philosophy of redemption there has been no agreement. But in this there has been agreement, that our hope of salvation, here and hereafter, is based solely upon the mediatorial work of Jesus Christ, the Son of God.

There recently came to my notice a very remarkable illustration of what Chalmers calls "the expulsive power of a new affection." It is said of Dr. Paxson, for many years connected with the American Sunday-School Union, that he was a very dull scholar at school. The teacher finally gave up in despair, and wrote his mother that the boy could not learn the multiplication table, and might as well be kept at home. It nearly broke his mother's heart. He found her crying bitterly. The curly-haired, blue-eyed, mischievous, fun-loving, but affectionate child wanted to know what the trouble was. And when she told him, he cried out: "Don't cry, you will break my heart; I did not suppose *you* cared, I did not think that *you* wanted me to learn the multiplication table. I will learn it by to-morrow night." And he did, to the amazement of the teacher, who came after a while to regard the boy as a mathematical prodigy. Love fulfilled the law. What the schoolmaster could not secure by authority, the mother secured by her tears. And the Law of God is our schoolmaster, leading us to Christ, the might of whose unspeakable love subdues us into obedience to the Law.

THE AUTHORITY OF THE BIBLE.

It may seem a matter of serious challenge to say, that a fourth great confession, in which there has been unbroken unanimity, is the pre-eminent and peculiar value of the Bible as a guide in religion, and as a record of the revelation of God to men. It may be objected that, on the one hand, the Roman Catholic communion does not recognize the infallible authority of Holy Scripture; and that, on the other hand, there are many in the ranks of Protestantism who by their critical methods have reduced the Old and New Testaments to a confused mass of fable and fraud. But this is an overstatement in both directions. The Roman Catholic Church is thoroughly orthodox on the doctrine of Scripture. The present Pope has proclaimed himself to be the advocate of the most strenuous theory of verbal and plenary inspiration. The Bible, for the Roman Church, is the Word of God. The debate between Rome and us concerns two things, the authority of tradition, and the organ of interpretation. The only authority acknowledged by us is that of Scripture. Rome claims coordinate and complementary authority for apostolic tradition, preserved in institutions and customs, of which there is no mention in the written documents of the New Testament. A second matter in debate concerns the right of private interpretation. We are committed to the doctrine of private judgment in religion, to the freest and most fearless study of the Bible by men of every class. Rome contends that the priesthood is the guardian of the faith, that Councils and Papal decrees determine what the Scriptures really teach, and that the decisions of the hierarchy must be accepted as final. We believe in an infallible book interpreted by fallible men; Rome believes in an infallible book interpreted by an order of infallible men. Such, too, is practically the doctrinal position of the Greek Church.

As for the claims of Protestant criticism of the Scriptures, however impatient we may be with it — and for the greater part it is, in my judgment, petty and shallow — it is only fair to say that many of the critics claim not to diminish the religious authority of the Bible, but only to modify the traditional notions of its inspiration and historical inerrancy. To use a somewhat inelegant figure, there is more bark than bite in this dog. It is only the frightened man who gets hurt. The doctrine of inspiration, as so conservative a theologian as the late Dr. Chalmers frankly admitted, has never been definitely formulated; and it may be doubted whether it ever can be. It really belongs to speculative divinity. The only practical question is whether the statements of fact and of doctrine, given in the Scriptures, are trustworthy and authoritative in the realm of faith and conduct. I am not aware that such authority is denied them, except by those who are avowedly hostile to Christianity, or by those who have hastily yielded to the clamor of the new critical school, and their attitude need not greatly concern us. The practical value of Scripture is universally acknowledged. We may as well let the critics alone. They will decimate each others ranks. There will not be a new Bible, nor will the old Bible pass away. The great body of the people will continue to read their Bibles in the same good old way. They have a feeling that the old prophets and apostles — Moses and Isaiah, Paul and John — knew vastly more about religion, and religious history, than the critics who are on a still hunt for Elohists, and Jahvists, and Redactors. And we may as well read our Bibles as Timothy was exhorted to read it, with the desire and purpose to be made wise unto salvation. I am not going to wait for the New Bible. I am sure it will be worthless, when it does come. The Old is not only good enough; it cannot be improved; and every attempt to reconstruct it has resulted in collapse. Universal Christendom stands firm on the Rock of Holy Scripture.

EVANGELIZATION.

Christendom is agreed in another confession, that the present life is the sphere within which the gospel is to secure its triumph. We are not to sit still, sing psalms, and wait for heaven. We are to do with our might what our hands find to do. We are to make our lives heavenly, and prepare the way of the Lord in all the earth. And the way of the Lord is righteousness, peace, and joy, in the Holy Ghost. Christ is to dwell in our hearts by faith, and so fashion us into His likeness; and, thus fashioned, we are to fill the earth with the word and power of His salvation. Christianity binds us to the immediate conquest of the world by the gospel. The missionary spirit is its beating heart, and animating breath. There is nothing for which I long so much, as a profound and universal revival of missionary enthusiasm, at home and abroad. The flag silences party clamor. The cross, as our banner of conquest, will draw our diverging lines together, and cement us into the only unity worth having. And in the earnest grapple with the world, we shall learn soonest what is primary and essential, and what is subordinate and incidental. Work will simplify and solidify our thinking. We have wasted our time in ornamenting, and polishing the scabbard, within which the sword has rusted, — let us draw the gleaming blade, and throw the sheath away!

THE ETERNAL GLORY.

And yet, our vision is not bounded by time. We preach Jesus, and the resurrection; the Risen Christ as the first-fruits of all that sleep, on land, and in the sea. Christianity lives, and moves, and has its being, in eternity,—in the eternity which never began, and which never ends. The God in whom we believe is from everlasting to everlasting. The Law which we honor can never become obsolete. It will remain, when heaven and earth shall have passed away. The Savior in whom we trust has conquered death, bringing life and immortality to light, showing us that corruption must put on incorruption, and the grave become the cradle of an endless life. The Risen Lord is our leader, whom we follow into the gloom of the sepulcher, that we may emerge with Him into the glory of the unending day. Everything in the Christian confession is keyed to immortality and eternal blessedness. There shall come an end to weakness and weariness, an end to pain and tears; while the songs of our pilgrimage shall swell into the unending psalm of victory and joy!

CONCLUSION.

That God is personal and living, that His law is sovereign and immutable, that Jesus Christ came to save sinners, that the Scriptures are able to make us wise unto salvation, that the kingdom of God is to cover the earth, and that our citizenship in it makes us heirs of eternal glory,—these are some of the things in which we are all agreed. They are the great things; and by that rule, let us walk!

CHAPTER VII.

THE INTEGRITY OF THE NEW TESTAMENT.

> "The testimony of the Lord is sure."
> —PSALM xix: 7.

THE nineteenth psalm naturally falls into two parts; the first dealing with the revelation of God in His works, the second with the revelation of God in His Word. The visible universe presents no object more prominent than the sun, whose light and heat are the universal and inexhaustible source of physical well being. We can conceive of no calamity more overwhelming and irremediable, than the sun's extinction. Horace Bushnell's vivid description of such a possible catastrophe will be recalled by every one who has read it: "Let the light of the morning cease and return no more, let the hour of morning come, and bring with it no dawn: the outcries of a horror-stricken world fill the air, and make, as it were, the darkness audible. The beasts go wild and frantic at the loss of the sun. The vegetable growths turn pale and die. A chill creeps on, and frosty winds begin to howl across the freezing earth. Colder, and yet colder, is the night. The vital blood, at length, of all creatures, stops congealed. Down goes the frost to the earth's center. The heart of the sea is frozen; nay, the earthquakes are themselves frozen in, under their fiery caverns. The very globe itself, too, and all the fellow planets that have lost their sun, are become mere balls of ice, swinging silent in the darkness. Such is the light, which revisits us in the silence of the morning."

A similar prominence for man's higher life is frequently attributed to the Word of God. It is a lamp. It is light. It is the sun of the soul, giving light and life, ministering illumination and inspiration. It is represented as the fixed and immovable center of Divine truth, "forever settled in heaven." It provides the basis of an infallible certainty; just as the sun, by its invisible, but constant and efficient, energy, secures the stability of the planetary system. Such a basis there must be somewhere, if our religious convictions and hopes are to be anything more than the creations of individual and diseased fancy; and it would seem as if we must choose between an infallible consciousness, an infallible church, and an infallible book. The first gives us rationalism or mysticism, in which every man is regarded as either hopelessly ignorant, or virtually omniscient; the second gives us traditionalism or Romanism, in which we believe upon the authority of the church, and of its constituted officers, whose duty it is to define the faith, and to save our souls; the third is the platform of evangelical Protestantism, which exalts the Bible above the individual and the Church, confessing it to be the sole and sufficient authority for man's religious faith and conduct.

That affirmation forces Biblical criticism to the very front of the Christian Sciences, and commits the Protestant household of faith to its most assiduous and enthusiastic cultivation. Not scholars alone, but every intelligent reader of the Bible, needs to know, on what ground he may affirm, without the slightest hesitation, that his hands turn the leaves of a book, whose origin dates to the times of inspired apostles and prophets; so that we may read it with the same eagerness as if we were hearing for ourselves the original message, or as if we locked arms with Abraham, Moses, Isaiah, Paul, and Christ Himself. The plain Christian accepts the Old Testament as inspired Scripture, upon the authority of Christ. We feel that it is safe for us to treat and use these older Scriptures, as He treated and used them. But we know Jesus Christ only through the gospels and the epistles. This practically narrows down the critical problem to the New Testament. Is the New Testament the literary record of the ancient and apostolic testimony and interpretation, or is it the product of a later age, mingling fact and fiction, giving us revelation in the garb of legend and romance? What evidence have we that our New Testament was in the hands of the Christian Churches of the year 100, when the last one of the apostles had just been buried by loving hands? A brief consideration of the answer to that question may fitly bring our present study to a close.

THE PRESUMPTIVE EVIDENCE.

There is, first of all, what may be called the presumptive evidence. The New Testament is in our hands, and it commands a reverence which is unique, and which no other books share with it. There is no extravagance in saying that this one little volume outweighs in importance, in the judgment of millions, all other literary treasures combined. It goes where no other book gains entrance, and no other book can drive it out. And yet, it is a stranger in the great literatures of the world. It is not the product of Hellenic genius, nor of German speculation, nor of French art, nor of Anglican thought. Its preeminence cannot be accounted for by any national enthusiasm; for the nation from whose great souls it sprang, is the one nation which thus far has deliberately scorned its message. We have received it at the hands of the Jew, whom we despise and shun. It is an alien book which has conquered us, and for which we are prepared to die.

These are facts which must be accounted for. There was a time when the book was not. **How** came it to be? And not only must the book be accounted for, but there must be some good and sufficient explanation of the singular reverence and affection, which this little volume has provoked, among so many peoples, and through so many centuries, in hovels and palaces, in lowly cottages and seats of learning. The cause certainly must be equal to the effect. And it is not simply the book which must be traced to its adequate literary origin, but the unique and unshared power which it has wielded must be associated with those who were concerned in its production. They could not have been weak men. They could not have been false men. They could not have been dreamers and deceivers. They could not have been romancers and enthusiasts. For their words have made men strong, and true, and clear-visioned, and intensely practical. If we may judge the tree by its fruits, we may and must assume that whatever claims the New Testament makes as to authorship, and time of composition, and credibility of contents, are practically beyond all reasonable challenge.

There are some who argue as if time had not settled some things. They speak in the tone of universal denial, and challenge the faith of the church in the New Testament, as if that challenge had not been met a hundred times before. Christianity does not evade the challenge, but it would seem as if eighteen hundred years of controversy, of heroic suffering and costly sacrifice, ought to have given to the New Testament an assured standing. Its claims must be accepted as presumptively true, unless they can be shown to be false. The burden of proof rests upon those who deny or doubt its integrity or credibility. Denial or doubt, in the face of this long tenure of power, and in contradiction of what the book itself affirms, is little less than impertinence. It is the audacity of insolence. It might as well be denied that Milton wrote "Paradise Lost;" for if he did not write it, as he claims to have done, the critic is bound to make good his denial by showing who did write it. If it should be said that no one now living could vouch for Milton's having lived, and written the poem, and that the original manuscript could not be produced, men would wonder whether the critic were sane.

Here, now, are certain books or pamphlets, some of them attributed by ancient and uniform tradition to Matthew, Mark, and Luke, and others claiming to have been written by Paul, and John, and James, and Peter. The presumption is that they were written by these men, unless the contrary can be clearly established beyond all possible question. Denial means nothing; demonstration must be forthcoming. The New Testament must stand as an authentic book, as the creation and the legacy of the apostolic age, which it claims to be, unless the contrary can be made out; and such a thing has never been done. The literature of the first three centuries of the Christian era has been ransacked, through and through, with microscopic minuteness, hundreds of times, and no other place can be assigned to the New Testament, than the one which it claims for itself. It fits into the first century; and it fits nowhere else. This amounts to a practical demonstration, that its claim is true.

THE DIRECT EVIDENCE.

The case might be made to rest here. But we may proceed to the direct evidence, that the New Testament belongs to the first and apostolic century of our era, which evidence is wonderfully varied and abundant. The printing press was used for the first time in the middle of the fifteenth century, more than four hundred years ago; and it surely needs not to be proved that the New Testament has suffered from no additions or mutilations, since the time when type secured its fixedness. But at that time it was already an old book, whose manuscript copies had been multiplied by the labors of monks, to whose industry we owe the preservation of the treasures of ancient literature.

The original parchments of the New Testament books have perished, and the earliest transcriptions were probably destroyed during the Domitian persecution. But the same thing is true of Homer's poetry, of Plato's philosophy, of the entire range of Greek and Roman letters. Few manuscripts of Greek or Roman classics are older than the ninth or tenth century of our era. There is one of Virgil dating from the fourth century; but the oldest manuscript copies of Æschylus and of Sophocles date from the tenth, and of Tacitus from the eleventh, century. The oldest complete copy of Homer is from the thirteenth century. And the number of such manuscripts is very limited, as compared with those containing the New Testament.

The extant New Testament manuscripts fall into two classes, the cursive and the uncial. Cursive manuscripts are those which are written in a running hand, and in small letters, while uncial manuscripts are written exclusively in capital letters. Of these two classes, the uncial manuscripts are the oldest. Of the cursive manuscripts, written between the ninth and the fifteenth centuries, there are nearly a thousand, thirty of them containing the entire New Testament; six hundred containing the gospels; two hundred containing the Acts and the Catholic Epistles; three hundred containing the Epistles of Paul; and one hundred containing the Revelation of John. Beside these, there are eighty-three uncial manuscripts, dating from the fourth to the ninth centuries. The ninth century is the dividing line between uncial and cursive writing. Of the eighty-three uncial manuscripts, the oldest is the Codex Vaticanus, preserved in the Vatican library at Rome, and dating from the year 325. Next in age, and fully equal in importance, is the Codex Sinaiticus, named from the convent at Sinai, where Tischendorf discovered and rescued it in 1859, preserved in the Imperial library at St. Petersburg, and dating from the year 340. The Codex Alexandrinus, presented by the Patriarch Cyril Lucar of Constantinople, in 1628, to King Charles I., and preserved in the British Museum, was probably written in Alexandria in the fifth century. The Codex Regius, preserved in Paris, also belongs to the fifth century, and was written in Alexandria. These four manuscripts are the oldest, and occupy the first rank. Of these, the Codex Sinaiticus alone is complete; but the Codex Vaticanus is the oldest, and is regarded by most critics as highest in authority. Beside these manuscripts, there are over four hundred Lectionaries, of which about seventy are uncials, containing the Scripture lessons read in public worship, compiled from the Gospels and the Epistles. The total number of all manuscripts is over seventeen hundred, dating from A. D. 325 to 1450, from which the present text of the New Testament has been compiled, by the most careful and critical comparison and sifting, a task begun by Erasmus in 1516, and continued until our own time. Three hundred and eighty years of scholarly research have been devoted, with unflagging patience and enthusiasm, to this work. It may be doubted whether the discovery of the original autographs would prove to be of any material value for the correction of the existing text.

The critical or direct evidence is simply overwhelming, when compared with that on the ground of which we accept the Greek and the Roman classics. And the earliest manuscript is substantially the same as our New Testament. The various readings, which amount to over a hundred thousand, are for the greater part insignificant, corresponding to typographical errors, and mistakes in proof-reading, in our time; and not more than four hundred materially affect the narrative; while not a single one modifies, in the slightest degree, any doctrine of the Christian Faith. In fact, the various readings have been an incalculable help to critical scholars, as by comparison they have provided the means of their own correction, while they have served to show how widely and numerously manuscript copies of the New Testament must have been in circulation, from a very early day.

THE CORROBORATIVE EVIDENCE.

The corroborative evidence for the fact that the New Testament belongs to the literature of the first century of the Christian era, and so gives us an authoritative account of the origin of Christianity, is hardly less varied, abundant, and convincing. Our literatures are, for the most part, limited in their reputation and influence. Even a national circulation is the exceptional fact. When a book appears in a translation, and wins its way among readers of another tongue, the tribute to its worth is unmistakable. Such translations of the New Testament are found to have existed in Armenia, in Syria, in Northern

Africa, in Ethiopia, and in Germany, at a very early day, antedating the oldest preserved uncial manuscript. While, however, the translations or versions carry us farther back than the oldest uncial manuscripts, we are indebted for our knowledge of the versions themselves to copies, not one of which is as old as the fourth century. These versions, or translations, were numerous, and are located in widely separated centers. The most important are the Old Latin, current in Northern Africa, and dating from the middle of the second century; the Peshito, or Syriac, very famous and influential, justly called "the queen of ancient versions," still read in the Syrian churches, and held in the highest esteem by scholars for its accurracy and force, dating in its present form from the fourth century, the present form being, however, a careful revision of an older version; the Egyptian or Coptic versions, of which there are three, in different dialects, independent of each other, and dating from the second century; the Ethiopic or Abyssinian, praised by Dillmann for its fidelity and smoothness, and dating from the fourth century; the Gothic, translated by Ulphilas, the apostle of Christianity to the Goths, invaders of Rome and destroyers of its proud empire, and dating from the fourth century; the Armenian version, dating from the fifth century; and the famous Vulgate, the first book ever printed, at Mayence, by Gutenburg and Fust, in 1455, translated from the Hebrew and the Greek by Jerome in 405, displacing the Old Latin Version, and for nearly fifteen hundred years the recognized translation of the Roman Catholic Church.

Here, then, there are translations, and even revisions, within one and two hundred years after John's death, and these from widely separated quarters, undertaken and carried through independently, to meet an urgent demand. These versions appear in rapid succession in Northern and Central Africa, in Syria, in the mountains of Armenia, along the northern shores of the Black Sea; and wherever they appear, the apostolic origin and authority are assumed.

Again, the controversial and explanatory literature, which a book provokes, helps us in estimating its value, and locating its first appearance.

The early Christian literature, in sermons, and commentaries, and decrees of councils, and theological treatises, makes a very respectable library, and renders unanimous and enthusiastic reverence to the apostolic origin and authority of the New Testament. It has been said that it would be easy, from this literature, to reproduce the substance of the New Testament, if every copy should be destroyed. In fact, the imperfect text of the Old Latin or Itala version, which circulated in Northern Africa as early as the middle of the second century, has been made practically complete by the help of quotations found in the writings of Tertullian, Cyprian, Hilary, Ambrose, Jerome, Augustin, and others. The Greek Testament lies in the heart of the early Christian literature, as Luther's Bible lies at the heart of German literature, as our own Bible lies at the heart of English literature. From these literatures both Bibles could be restored, without great difficulty, if every printed copy should be destroyed.

The brief tracts of the Apostolic Fathers, written between A. D. 80 and 125, assume the existence of the New Testament. The Didache, or

Teaching of the Twelve Apostles, discovered in the library of the Jerusalem Monastery, by the Metropolitan Bryennios, in 1873, and edited by him in 1883, assigned by Dr. Schaff to A. D. 90–100, is a most impressive witness to the "Gospel" as the source of authoritative teaching. As early as the middle of the second century we find Tatian, a famous rhetorician of Syria, editing a Harmony of the Four Gospels, as the only authentic and authoritative sources of our Lord's life. Passing from Syria to France, the works of Irenæus, of Lyons, who died in A. D. 190 or 202, and the letter of Polycarp, the martyr of Smyrna, who died in 155, and who was a personal pupil of the apostle John, as we learn from the testimony of Irenæus, who had seen and heard Polycarp in the latter's old age, conduct us to the very margin of the apostolic period. Clement and Origen were famous teachers of theology, in Alexandria, between A. D. 190 and 254, and had been preceded by Pantænus. Origen was one of the most learned of men, and a most prolific author, Jerome saying of him that he had written more than "other men read;" and among his works are commentaries on nearly every book of the Old and the New Testament. Alexandria had a school of Christian Theology as early as A. D. 180. Another theological school was founded at Antioch about A. D. 300, and became very celebrated. A third school was founded at Edessa, about A. D. 360, which trained the preachers for Mesopotamia and Persia, for a hundred years. There is much more of similar evidence, but enough has been adduced to show how abundant, solid, and convincing, is the evidence upon which we receive the gospels as recording the history of Christ, and the epistles as authoritative apostolic expositions of His ministry and mission. And to this corroborative evidence, from the literature of the first four centuries, might be added the liturgical evidence, embodied in Christian hymns and confessions, in the rude inscriptions upon the tombs of those who died in the faith, in the unbroken observation of the Christian Sabbath as a day of worship, of the Sacraments as instituted and enjoined by Christ, and of Easter as the annual commemoration of our Lord's resurrection from the dead.

THE EVIDENCE FROM IMPRESSION.

It is permissible for a man to testify on his own behalf, and to challenge the keenest cross-examination. It is perilous to invite the test; but for a thoroughly upright man it affords the opportunity of the most signal vindication. A truthful witness carries conviction and confidence in his tone and bearing. Bluster and boisterousness cannot make good the want of sincerity and of simple truthfulness. The New Testament is invested and pervaded with a simplicity, a directness, a transparency, a moral purity, and a spiritual loftiness, which convincingly attest its truthfulness. In these respects it stands conspicuously superior to the literature immediately following it. The apocryphal gospels condemn themselves by their puerility. Even the best of the Apostolic Fathers only repeat the commonplaces of Christian teaching; the New Testament is as manly and direct, as it is original and profound.

THE EVIDENCE FROM EXPERIENCE.

This practical argument is only carried one step farther, and to its legitimate goal, when it is made personal. The Christ, of whom the New Testament speaks, and who declared that Moses, the Prophets, and the Psalms, heralded His advent, death, and resurrection, is the Risen and Exalted Christ. We know Him through the historical record, but that record is the open door through which we pass into His living, personal presence. The historical knowledge, which we have of Him, carries us into invisible, but real and personal, fellowship with Him, as the river's current carries us into the sea. The record declares Him to be a Prince and a Savior, exalted to give repentance and remission of sins unto all who call upon Him. He is with us, and our Advocate in heaven. This leaves the way open to a personal verification of the record. Without any familiarity with the critical evidence, as outlined above, the reader may convince himself whether these things are so, or not. And Christian experience, with jubilant unanimity, adds its testimony to the sovereign and saving power of Jesus Christ. Nor, because the record passes into experience, while the experience confirms the record, is this arguing in a circle.

For, both the record, and the experience, have their source in Jesus Christ. His life on earth, the record sketches in outline, with outlook into the heavenly ministry; the ministry in heaven, and by the Spirit, He attests as real, in personal Christian experience, and thereby the certainty of the earthly record is confirmed. Upon Him, as Rock and Cornerstone, the Church is built; and the gates of Hades shall not prevail against her. Nero applied the torch, and Celsus sharpened his pen; but the Carpenter of Nazareth brought the Roman eagles to his feet. There can come no fiercer baptism of fire than that through which the ante-Nicene Church passed. And the issue of that early baptism is prophetic of all the future. The New Testament stands unimpeached and unimpeachable. It makes immutable the historic place and mission of Jesus Christ in the world. He is its invisible, but mighty and immortal King. To Him shall every knee bow. And as men bow to Him in increasing numbers, and with spontaneous joy, they will accept His estimate, and imitate His use, of the Ancient Scriptures, which for twenty years have been the target of an unparalleled bitter criticism. The smoke of battle will clear away, and the Old Book will emerge without a scar!

CONCLUDING WORD.

And now, I propose to take my readers into my confidence. Some, perhaps, will feel that the discussion has been fragmentary, and somewhat discursive. No one is more fully aware of that, than am I. It would have been easy to multiply these pages five and ten-fold. But the literature upon this subject is so great, that I may be excused for having touched only upon a few salient points, limiting myself to such as are most outstanding. Others may wonder that my pen has been so pointed and pungent. They may be surprised at my passionate intensity. And my heart is hot within me; but my head is cool, my eye is clear, and my hand is steady. To me, at least, an assault upon the integrity, and the historical credibility, of the Scriptures, is tenfold more serious than a denial of Divine inspiration. Give me a *true* book, and I am content. Give me a book which, in part or entire, is on a level with Æsop's fables, and while it may amuse me for an hour, I cannot take it seriously as a guide to heaven.

The passionate intensity with which I have written is due, not only to the supreme importance of the matter in debate, but also to the fierce personal mental struggle, through which I have passed during the last dozen years. I have been in the crushing coils of this critical anaconda, and know what the fight for life means. Less than twenty years ago, the revolutionary criticism made its appearance in our higher institutions of learning. It was unknown in my seminary days. It is all the rage now. Theology has been thrust into the back-ground, and the critic is in the saddle. He will not stay there long, for already the steed is becoming unmanageable. And when the new criticism first appeared, I ignored it. I did not believe the enemy ever would come within rifle range, and so I was not disturbed. But that which at first was only a rustle in the top leaves of the trees, swept downward and forward, and with increasing velocity. I kept my feet, and waited. At last, eight years ago, I could stand it no longer and I determined that the issue must be fairly and squarely met. I girded myself for the task. I took down my neglected Hebrew Bible, and plodded through its every line; once, and again, and yet again, — the Pentateuch a good many times. Meanwhile, the agony grew apace. Many a day was spent in restless pacing in my study; many a night was without any sleep, except the sleep of exhaustion. It seemed to me as if the Old Testament were slipping away from me. I dreaded to open it, and I dared not shut it. The darkness seemed growing denser. On I pressed, and stumbled, sometimes nearly losing my footing. The eddy became a maelstrom, whose hissing and whirling waters threatened to suck me into their cavernous depths. None knew my agony, for I bore it in silence. And Sunday after Sunday I went into my pulpit, to preach the gospel, while my heart was ready to break. I had lost my childhood faith, and there was none to take its place. The language of the first half of the twenty-second psalm is none too strong to describe the agony of those years.

But there came a time when I cried with the psalmist: "GNANITHANI; *Thou hast heard me!*" God drew me out of the engulfing waters, out of the pit and the miry clay, set my feet upon the rock, established my goings, and put a new song into my mouth. Be it eddy or whirlpool, I am out of both; and my feet are planted where the waters hiss and swirl, without so much as dashing their spray upon my footing. I have unlearned much. There are many things about which I have come to be indifferent, which I once regarded as essential. I have no words to waste upon questions of infallibility and inerrancy. Chronologies and genealogical tables have ceased to trouble me. Alleged discrepancies are no more to me than a few drops of rain on a radiant June day. The sun shines, and is regnant, for all that. The dispute, whether inspiration is verbal or noetic, mechanical or dynamic, partial or plenary, has lost its interest for me. Two things I know: *that the Bible is God's Book; and that it is true.* I smile when I hear men disputing about the phrases: "*The Bible is the Word of God,*" and "*The Word of God is in the Bible.*" I believe both, as I believe body and soul constitute a man. The message of God is the eternal soul; the history is the body in which that soul lives, and moves, and through which that soul acts. The message is infallible and eternal; *the history is true.* That is my confession. And I say frankly, that the message to me would not be infallible, did I believe the history false and fabricated. Nor, in the logical argument, do I prove the history true, because the message is divine; but the message retains for me its eternal and inspiring authority, because I am sure the history is true. The shafts of the destructive criticism fall wide of the mark. The logic assumes what it tries to prove. Its advocates pride themselves upon being radical, and class themselves as scientific critics, speaking of their opponents as conservatives, and labelling them as traditional. The radical is one who goes to the roots of things, and this is what the conservatives do. I deny the right of destructive criticism to the boast of being scientific. Science has respect for facts, for all the facts, and for the facts as found. Nothing can be more unscientific than the procedure of the Wellhausen school. It throws the material into hopeless confusion. It mutilates the facts. It deals in wholesale charges of bad faith, and of fraud. Its true designation is destructive criticism, and the new reading which it gives of the Biblical history is unworthy any serious man's consideration. It is a tragedy for the earnest man. It is a roaring farce for the skeptic. It gives pain to the believer. It invites the scorn of the unbeliever. It helps nobody. It tears the Bible into shreds, and dumps the book bodily into the literary ash-barrel. And that method is inviting sharp and sure defeat. To my eyes, at least, the swords have broken at the hilt, and the lances have snapped in the hands of those who have hurled them. The Scriptures are coming out of the smoke and fury of the battle, without a scar, and without the smell of fire upon their garments.

It is only my personal testimony; and it must pass for what it is worth. But I am jubilant in spirit. I am not disturbed by what fifty or sixty men, who assume to have the monopoly of scholarship, say. I have listened to them and they have not convinced me. I have sifted their learning and their logic, and found both wanting. They will laugh at my audacity, and treat me with the silence of contempt. But I do not assume the role of a specialist. They do not care for me; and I have ceased to care for them. I have been taking lessons from a better teacher. I have simply voiced my personal testimony, the outcome of a bloody sweat. My experience is something which cannot be taken away from me; and it has come to me, not in cloistered chambers, but in the arena where truth is a matter of life and death. I have fought my battle, and under God, I have gained my triumph. And, in these pages, I have spoken, not to the few, but to the many; to the thousands, who are dazed and bewildered, and to whom, perhaps, these words may prove to be a word of cheer and of courage.

For Bunyan tells us that when Christian came to the River, he began to sink, crying out: "I sink in deep waters; the billows go over my head; all his waves go over me." Whereupon, his good friend Hopeful answered: "Be of good cheer, my brother; I feel the bottom, and it is good." Then fell there upon Christian a great horror and darkness, so that he could not see before him. But, presently, *"Christian found good ground to stand upon, and so it followed that the rest of the river was but shallow; thus they got over."*

"The firm foundation of God standeth!" —II. Tim. ii: 19.

NOTE.

After the preceding pages had gone to press, the first volume of Professor Adolf Harnack's "The Chronology of the Old Christian Literature," came into my hands. It is fresh from the Leipzig press. It is a book of nearly 750 pages; and is, of course, exact and massive in its learning. It is not the work of a novice. Harnack is forty-six years old, has made early Christian history a specialty for twenty-five years, has held chairs in the universities of Leipzig, Giessen, and Marburg, and is at present the great shining light in Berlin. He is the leader of the school of Ritschl, at present dominant on the Continent, which insists upon eliminating all speculative elements from theology. Harnack's influence in the leading universities of England and America is great. His latest and ripest contribution is all the more remarkable, because even in Germany his orthodoxy has been fiercely assailed. He does not pose as the advocate of any school, for the Ritschlian method not only discards metaphysics in theology, but also denies the right of philosophy to meddle with the materials of history. Harnack insists that history must be permitted to tell its own story, and that its story must stand.

In his preface to the book above named, Harnack outlines the present state of New Testament criticism, and sums up briefly the results to which his studies have led him. I am sure that my readers will welcome the following translated extracts, which are from the original:

"There was a time,—the general public has not even yet passed out of it—when the oldest Christian literature, including that of the New Testament, was regarded as a tissue of deceptions and frauds. That time is past. For science, that time was an episode; during which much was learned, and after which much will have to be forgotten. But the results to which the following investigations lead, go beyond the moderate school in their reactionary direction. The oldest literature of the church, considered as historical writing, is in the main points, and in the majority of its details, true and trustworthy.

"Baur and his school once contended, that an intelligent and reliable sketch of the development of primitive Christianity could be drawn, only by surrendering, for the major part of the ancient Christian literature, the evidence of the writings themselves, and the testimony of tradition; and by dragging down the date of these writings several centuries. The presuppositions of the school of Baur, it may now be said, have been universally given up; but there remains, in the criticism of the old Christian writings, an indefinite distrust, a treatment such as proceeds from an irritated lawyer, or which, at all events, may be described as that of a third-rate and petty school-master.

"The last twenty years have been marked by retrograde judgment. I am not afraid, or ashamed, of the word '*retrograde;*' for things should be called by their right names, and in the criticism of the sources of primitive Christianity, we are unquestionably moving backwards towards tradition; for the chronological boundaries, within which tradition has fixed the documents, is in all main points, from the epistles of Paul to Irenæus, correct, and compels the historian to abandon all theories of historical development, which deny these boundaries. Only a few weeks ago, a Dutch theologian, who recognizes the boundaries within which tradition has fixed the primitive Christian documents, said to me that he had despaired of sketching a natural history of primitive Christianity, and was compelled to believe in a supernatural history.

"The time will come, and it is already upon us, when the historico-literary problems of primitive Christianity will cease to command attention, because it will be universally acknowledged that tradition speaks with authority. If the following pages shall contribute their part to recall confidence in the chronological boundaries, within which the primitive Christian literature is delivered to us, and to intensify the same, and so to transfer attention from literary problems to historical problems, their highest aim will have been secured. In the realm of history, not in the realm of literary criticism, lie the problems of the future."

The Germans speak of great books as "epoch-making." This book marks an epoch. It is a distinct, unqualified repudiation of the Higher Criticism in its assaults upon the integrity and the credibility of the New Testament. It is a straight-forward declaration, from the foremost scholar of Europe, that historical research supports the testimony of tradition. It announces, in decisive terms, that the battle of more than sixty years has ended in the hopeless rout of the critics. The New Testament has stood the test. Many of us knew it long ago; but Harnack has driven the last nail into the coffin. Baur is discredited by the most commanding voice of our time. Scholarship comes back to the faith of the nursery. The great have surrendered to the lowly. The foolishness of God has triumphed. The cottages have conquered the universities. It may well inspire us all with new courage and hope. The firm foundation of God standeth! For the critical postulates of the school of Wellhausen are identical with those of the school of Baur. They have been discredited in the region of the New Testament literature, which emerges unharmed from the keen dissection. Not a nerve has been severed, not a drop of blood has been drawn. The edge of the knife has left no mark. And the surgery will prove as harmless upon the Old Testament. *That* is not, any more than the New Testament, "a tissue of deceptions and frauds." The "supernatural history" recorded in it, will have to be believed. The time is coming, and it may be nearer than we think, when the literary problems of the Old Testament "will cease to command attention, because it will be universally acknowledged that tradition speaks with authority."

I said that, if I lived twenty years longer, I expected to see the school of Wellhausen laid out for solitary burial, with none to mourn its departure. From across the sea, and from the Royal University of Berlin, a new tone smites my ear, and it sounds like the tolling of the bell! Can it be that the end has come? It seems so; and it certainly cannot be very far off! And when the tolling dies away, the Church of God will prize her Bible more than ever!

www.ingramcontent.com/pod-product-compliance
Lightning Source LLC
Chambersburg PA
CBHW020807230426
43666CB00007B/897